THE USBORNE BOOK OF DRESSING UP

Edited by Cheryl Evans and Paula Borton
Designed by Ian McNee
Illustrated by Chris Chaisty   Photographs by Ray Moller

Contents

Face painting	1
Masks	33
Fancy dress	65

First published in 1993. Usborne Publishing Ltd., Usborne House, 83-85, Saffron Hill, London EC1N 8RT, England. Copyright © 1993 Usborne Publishing Ltd. The name Usborne and the device are Trade Marks of Usborne Publishing Ltd. All rights reserved. No part of this publication may be reproduced, stored in a retrieval system or transmitted in any form or by any means, electronic, mechanical, photocopying, recording or otherwise, without the prior permission of the publisher. Printed in Portugal.

NORFOLK LIBRARY AND INFORMATION SERVICE	
SUPPLIER	ASKEW
INVOICE No	164950
ORDER DATE	29.1.94
COPY No.	

J646.4

FACE PAINTING

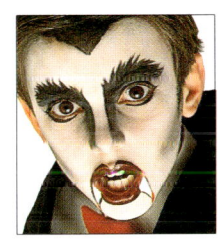

Chris Caudron and Caro Childs of Lococo

Contents

Ready to paint	2	Garlands	20
Mouse and rabbit	4	Sunset scene	22
Dogs	6	Designer patterns	24
Cats	8	Robot	26
Clowns	10	Kabuki	27
Witch and vampire	12	Owl	28
Skull and ghoul	14	Bat	29
Monsters	16	Party pieces	30
Butterflies	18	Portrait gallery	32

Ready to paint

To paint the exciting faces in this book you need water-based face paints. These cost a little more than other kinds, but give much better results. You can buy them from toy shops or theatrical costume suppliers (see page 32). Here's some more about how to start.

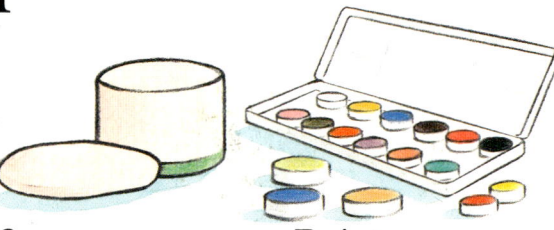

Sponges

You can use ordinary make-up sponges, or buy special, thick ones from face paint or theatrical suppliers. It is useful to have two or three sponges to use.

Paint

The paints come in single pots or a palette. They will not harm most skins, but always check for skin allergies first. They wash off with soap and water.

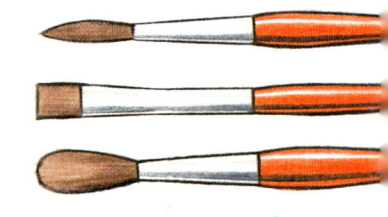

Paint brushes

You need at least one fine brush and one thick one. They may have flat or pointed ends, which make different shapes when you paint with them. Both kinds are useful.

Getting started

Wear old clothes, so it will not matter if you get paint on them (though it does wash off). Make sure your hands and the model's face are clean and dry. Tie back any hair that falls over your model's face. Here you can see the best way to set up to paint faces.

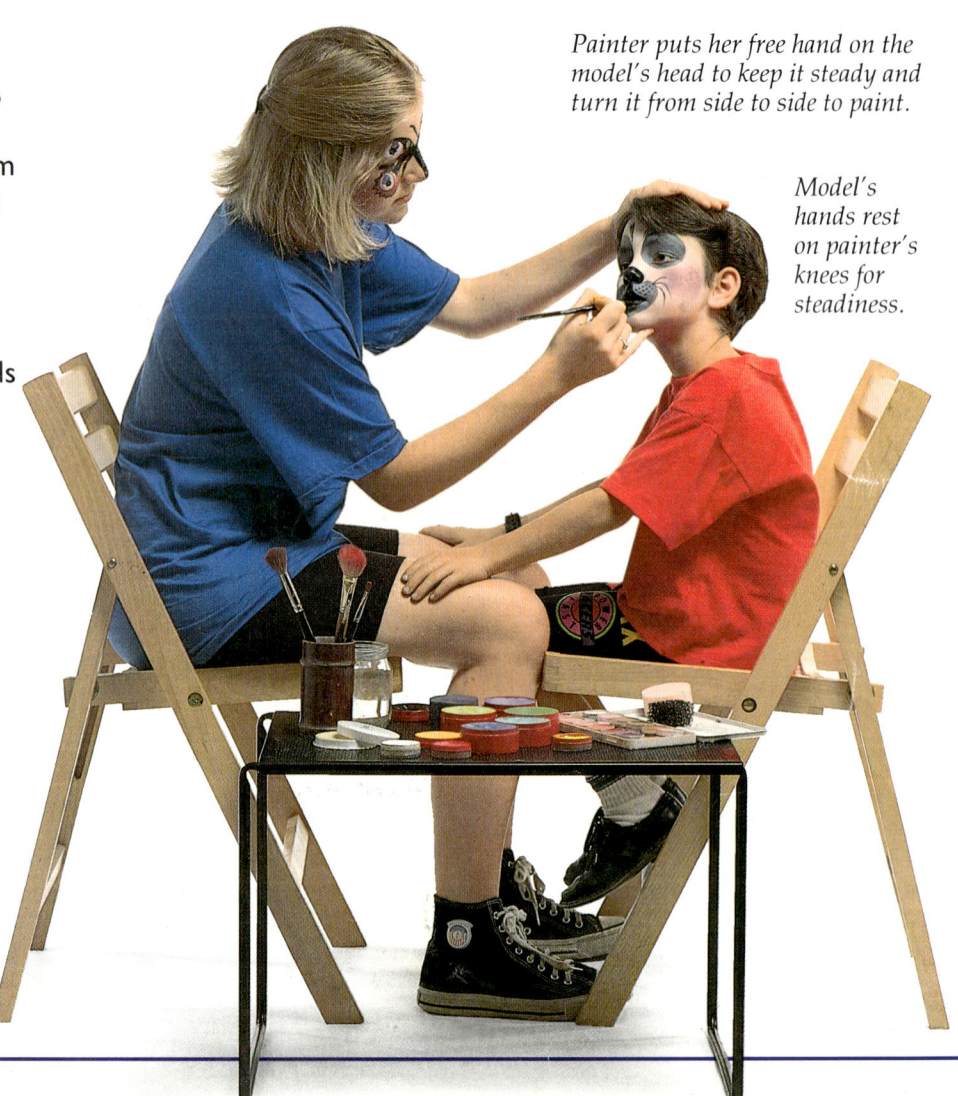

Painter puts her free hand on the model's head to keep it steady and turn it from side to side to paint.

Model's hands rest on painter's knees for steadiness.

Sit very close to your model, on chairs facing each other.

Have one set of knees outside of the other.

Place paints and water on a table near your painting hand.

2

Sponging a base

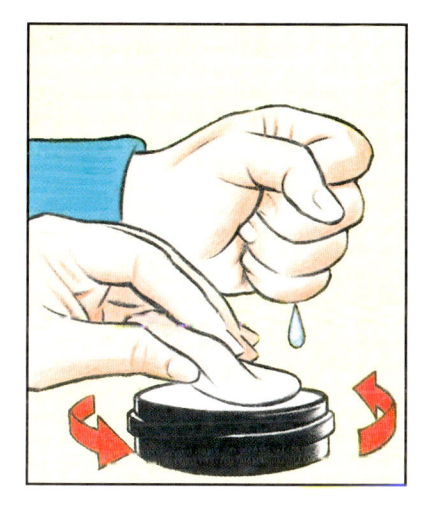

If it streaks, your sponge is too wet.

1. It is vital to learn how to sponge an even base. Wet a sponge and squeeze hard until no more drops come out. Rub the sponge lightly in circles over the paint.

2. Apply the paint evenly all over the face. Dab and push the sponge onto the face with a twist of the wrist. Don't try to sponge in long, dragging strokes.

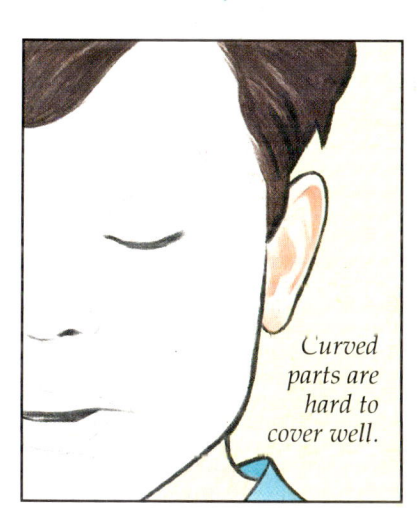

Curved parts are hard to cover well.

Paint right up to hair line.

3. Don't forget the eyelids. Ask the model to look up and work carefully close under his eyes. Dab well into the creases around the nose, mouth and eye corners.

4. Check that the base is neat and even all over. Turn the model's face gently to each side to check the paint on the chin line is not ragged. Correct it if it is.

Brush control

Hold the brush like a pencil, a little above the bristles.

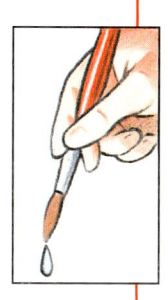

Get it really wet, then wipe and roll the bristles gently across the paint toward you.

Paint with the brush at a right angle to the face. (The red lines show you this angle).

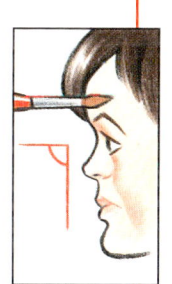

Lay the bristles flat on the face and press as you paint to make a thick line.

Lift the brush off and paint lightly with the tip to make a fine line or come to a point.

3

Mouse and rabbit

There are lots of animal faces you can paint. Try to find one that suits your model's face shape and hair. Some animals simply do not work well as their faces are not at all like people's - a horse, elephant or crocodile, for example.

Sugar mouse

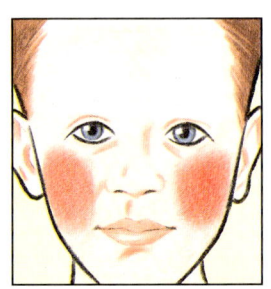

1. Sponge pink onto both cheeks. With white on a brush, paint a curve over each eyebrow. Fill in the shape down to the eye sockets, just below the eyebrows.

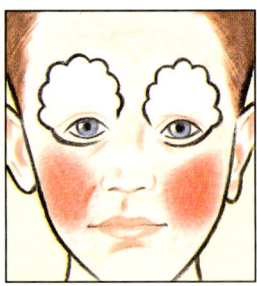

2. Now put black on your brush and do a wavy outline from one corner of the eye to the other, around the white curve. Streak a black line out under each eye.

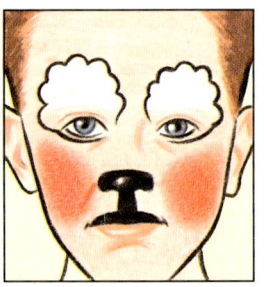

3. Paint the whole end of the nose black. Go between the nostrils, too. Paint a line from under the nose to the top lip black. Then do the top lip black.

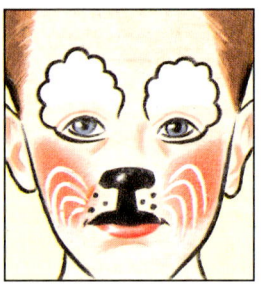

4. Paint black dots on each side of the line from the nose to the top lip. Now with white paint again, do whiskers curving down. Paint the bottom lip bright red.

Tips

Apply with a brush.

You can use pink make-up blusher in place of paint on the cheeks. Face paint suppliers sell other blusher shades.

Face paint is easily licked off lips. For pink or red lips, borrow or buy a lipstick to use. It will stay on longer.

4

Stripes go onto top lip.

Whiskers curve down

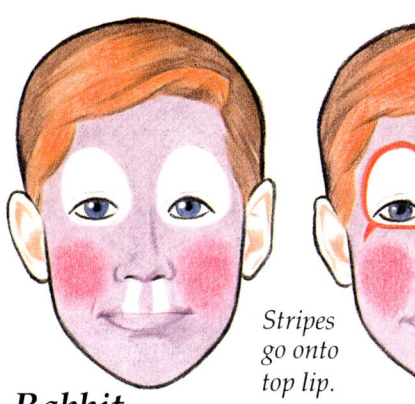

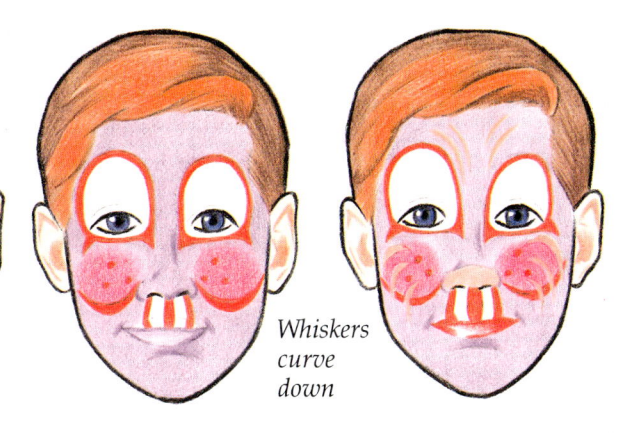

Rabbit

1. Sponge a mauve base and blush pink cheeks. Fill in a white arched shape above each eye and do two white stripes under the nose for teeth.

2. With red, paint smoothly around the white arches. Do a line under each eye that slopes down at both ends. Outline the white teeth.

3. Still with red, paint curves around the rosy cheeks, starting from the bottom corners of the nose. Add three dots on each cheek.

4. With pink, paint the end of the nose and curved whiskers which start from near the red dots. Paint two pink streaks up by each eyebrow.

Finger trick

Here's a way to do smooth brushstrokes. Hold the brush above where you want to start.

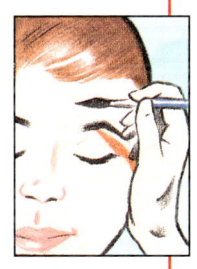

Find a place to put your little finger on the face nearby. Paint your line, keeping your finger still.

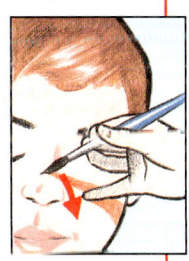

It may feel strange at first, but it will soon help you to paint confident lines.

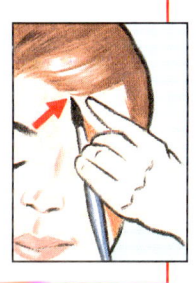

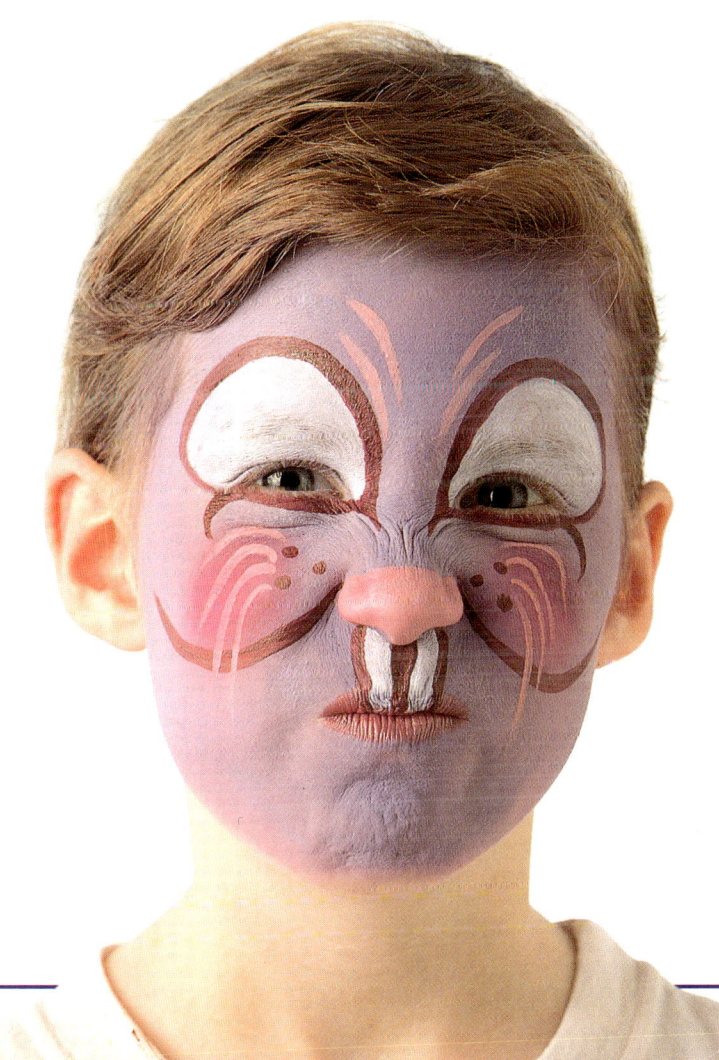

5

Dogs

Spotted dog

When you paint a dog, look at your model's face well before you start. Is it round and chubby or long and thin? Try to think what kind of dog it looks like. This one suits a small, round face.

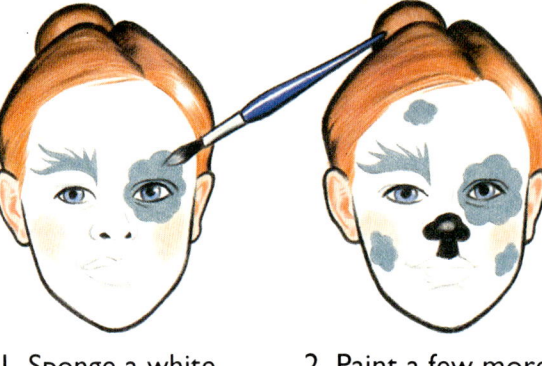

1. Sponge a white base. Add a little pink to each cheek. With a brushful of grey, paint a patch around one eye and a spiky eyebrow over the other eye.

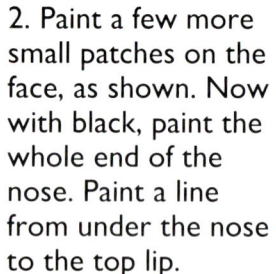

2. Paint a few more small patches on the face, as shown. Now with black, paint the whole end of the nose. Paint a line from under the nose to the top lip.

3. Fill the top lip in with black. Put three black dots on each side of the line under the nose and paint fine, black whiskers out onto each cheek. The ends curve down.

Arrange hair to look like dog's ears.

White streaks next to black whiskers make them stand out more.

4. Do a broad, red tongue over half of the lower lip and onto the chin. Fill in the rest of the lower lip with black and do a streak down the tongue when it's dry.

Technique tip

As a rule, add details from the top down, that is eyebrows first and mouth last. However, once you have paint on your brush, it's a good idea to use it wherever it is needed - do all the black bits you can at once, for example. It may break the rule, but saves rinsing the brush too much.

White-faced dog

For this dog you need brown paint. If you do not have any, you can make it by mixing on your sponge. Rub your sponge in black, then orange and test it on the back of your hand. To make it lighter, rub in some yellow or white.

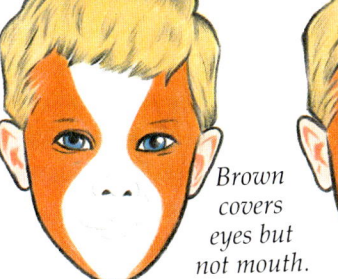

Brown covers eyes but not mouth.

1. Sponge a broad white stripe down the middle of the face. Then sponge a brown, curved shape down each side, like this. The brown overlaps the white.

2. With black on a brush, paint thick eyebrows and a line under each eye. Paint up the creases on each side of the nose to meet on top and fill in with black.

3. Paint a strip from under the nose to the top lip black. Fill the top lip in with black. Put dots to show where whiskers start on the muzzle on each side of the strip.

Ask your model to try making dog expressions.

Whiskers start near black spots.

4. Paint a red tongue over the bottom lip onto the chin, then do a black bottom lip, as for the patches dog. Do white whiskers curving onto each cheek.

Animal features

Many animals have a split upper lip and whiskers. Features like these help you to recognize them. Think of other typical features to use when you try more animals.

7

Cats

You can do lots of versions of this cat face. Look at real cats' markings to do pet cats, or look at pictures of the big, wild cats. Use your imagination to create bright fantasy cats.

Always sponge the middle of the cat's face a paler shade than the outside. This makes the face seem to come forward, like an animal's muzzle.

Shading makes these parts sink into face.

1. Sponge a base with a paler middle. Use a contrasting, darker paint to sponge shadows on the forehead and cheeks.

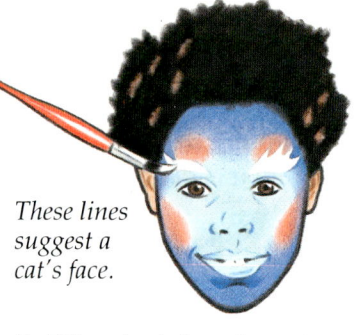

These lines suggest a cat's face.

2. Fill a thick brush with white. Paint whiskery face markings out along the eyebrows. See how to do this in the box below.

3. Paint down the smile lines from nose to lips. Curve up and out to a point on the cheeks. Do it a few times, curving sooner each time.

Eyebrow whiskers

Lay the brush down. Paint a line along the brow bone.

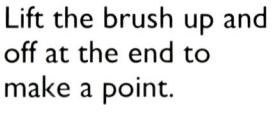

Lift the brush up and off at the end to make a point.

Repeat a few times. Lift the brush sooner each time.

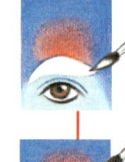

Add extra dots and streaks, if you like.

4. Fill in above the top lip with white, except for a strip under the nose. Using dark red, underline the eyes and outline the whiskers.

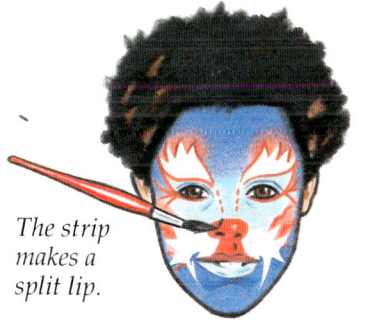

The strip makes a split lip.

5. Paint the end of the nose (under the tip, too), the strip you left below the nose, and the top lip in your contrasting red paint.

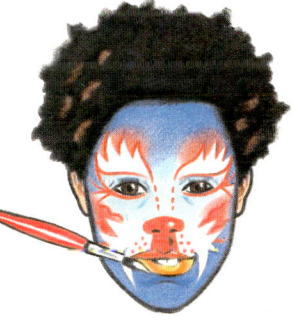

6. Put a few red whisker dots on the white patches above the top lip. Finally, paint the bottom lip gold.

Paint hands to match face, if you like.

Tiger (above)

Give a yellow tiger black stripes and sharp teeth. It is more important to suggest the animal's markings than to be strictly accurate.

Leopard (below)

Sponge a rounded white muzzle and chin on a yellow-brown base. Groups of brown spots suggest a leopard's hide.

Clowns

Traditionally, every clown invents his own face paint to please himself, so no two ever look the same.

Circus clown

The pictures below show you the basic way to paint a clown's face. Look at the big picture and the box on the right for more ideas.

Mouths

Curved up looks happy.

Curved down looks sad.

Paint a big mouth over and outside of the lips. The simplest one to do is a blobby, sausage shape.

Eyebrows

Curved brows

Shaggy brows

Paint eyebrows above the real ones. Happy clowns can have bright eyebrows. Black eyebrows look scarier.

Ask your model to look up as you paint under the eyes.

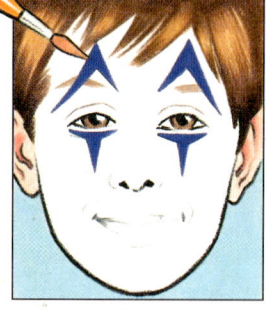

1. Sponge a white base. Paint thick eyebrows any shape you like. Underline the eyes and do a thin triangle down from the middle of each line.

Stars or spots are good.

2. Paint a red nose and a big mouth. This one goes out onto the cheeks and ends in big red dots. If you like, add more bright shapes.

This clown has thick, pointed eyebrows.

His eyelids are painted up to the eyebrows, with spots on.

Leave a streak of white in cheek dots to make them "shine".

Pierrot

Pierrot (say pee-air-oh) clowns are beautiful, but often sad. Take time to do a thorough, even, white base first. Then the few strong details show up well.

Tip

This face works best if the two sides are not quite the same: paint different eyebrow shapes in step 2.

The black hairband and painted point on the forehead suggest a Pierrot's black skull cap.

This mouth is painted narrow, with higher points and a more curved bottom lip than her real lips.

Leave a streak of white on the tear for "shine".

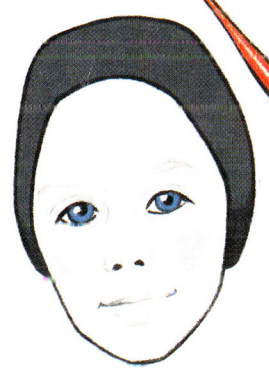

1. Carefully sponge a white base. Sponge or blush the cheeks lightly, with pale mauve or blue.

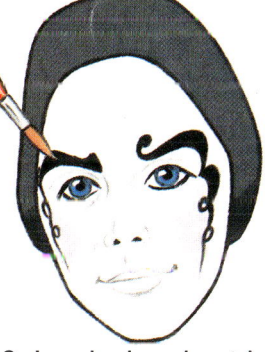

2. Load a brush with black paint to do fancy eyebrows. Curl them down onto the cheeks.

3. Paint a fine black line out under each eye. Outline a big teardrop shape under one eye only.

4. Paint the eyelids in a delicate shade up to the line of the eye socket. Do a gold tear and pink lips.

11

Witch and vampire

These eerie faces are good for witches, space aliens or supernatural creatures. Work on a really subtle base first, then add the details.

Changing shape

These effects look best on mean, lean faces. You can make any face look thinner by clever shading. Here's how you can do it.

1. Start with a creepy base such as white, green or mauve. Shading should be darker so sponge it with a little black, dark mauve or deep blue.

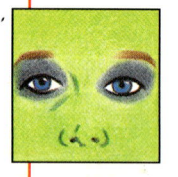

2. Shade the eye sockets. This makes the eyes seem to sink deeper.

3. Stroke the sponge down both sides of the nose so it looks bony.

4. Make the cheeks hollow by darkening under the cheekbones.

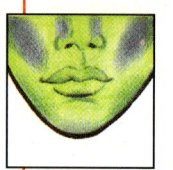

5. Shade the side edges of the chin.

Witch

Fluorescent green looks unearthly.

1. Sponge and shade a bony green face, as shown on the left. It would work just as well using blues or mauves.

Exaggerate eyebrow shape.

2. Pick a strong contrast for brushwork. Press and paint a line out along each brow bone. Lift the brush up at the end to make a point.

Join underline to brows, if you like.

Use a thin brush for spiky lines.

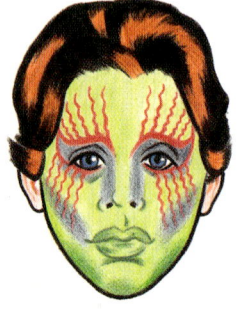

3. Sweep a line out under the eyes for emphasis. Paint spiky, wavy lines up from the eyebrows and down from the eye underline.

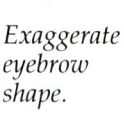

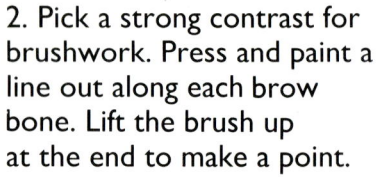

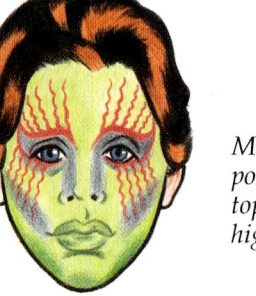

Make points of top lips higher.

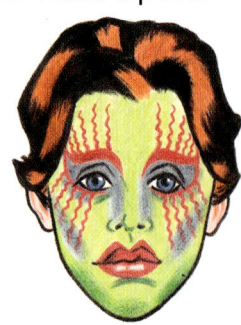

4. Paint the lips in your contrast shade. Tell your model to keep her mouth gently closed. Exaggerate the top lips and fill them in.

12

Vampire

Extend black down sides of nose.

1. Sponge a thorough white base. Shade it in grey (see left). With black on a brush, do wicked, shaggy eyebrows and underline the eyes.

Outline outside of lips.

2. With black, outline the lips and paint sharp fangs down from the corners of the top lip. When they dry, touch up the fangs with more white.

You can sponge black onto fair hair, if you like. It washes out.

3. When the fangs are dry again, add a discreet droplet of scarlet blood on their tips. Fill the lips in with deep red paint.

Hag

To paint an evil old hag, sponge a pale base with dark shading. Then ask your model to screw up her face. See where creases appear and paint along them with fine grey and brown lines. Do lots of small lines off the main ones and add some white lines for highlight. Do shaggy grey eyebrows and thin lines across the lips.

Stipple (page 23) sideburns, if you like.

Brush hair back and paint a black "widow's peak" on forehead.

Skull and ghoul

These are faces to frighten your friends or wear to a scary party. There are more party ideas on pages 30-31.

Skull

1. Sponge a white base. With a very dry sponge, dab just a little green around the edges, to look like mold.

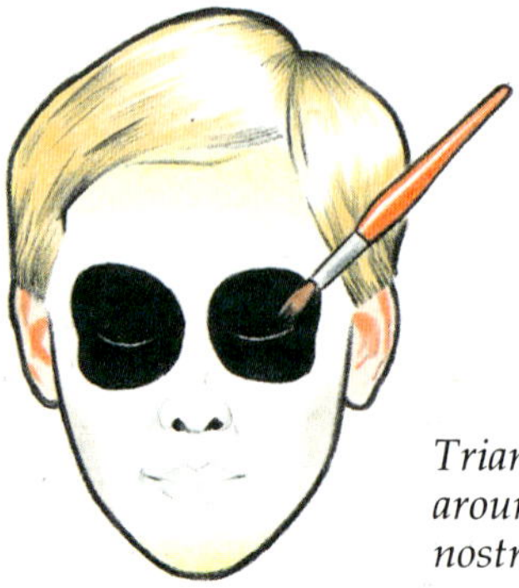

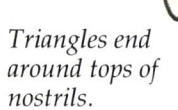

Ask model to close his eyes while you paint his eyelids.

2. Sponge grey shadows under the cheekbones. Load a brush with black and paint a circle around each eye.

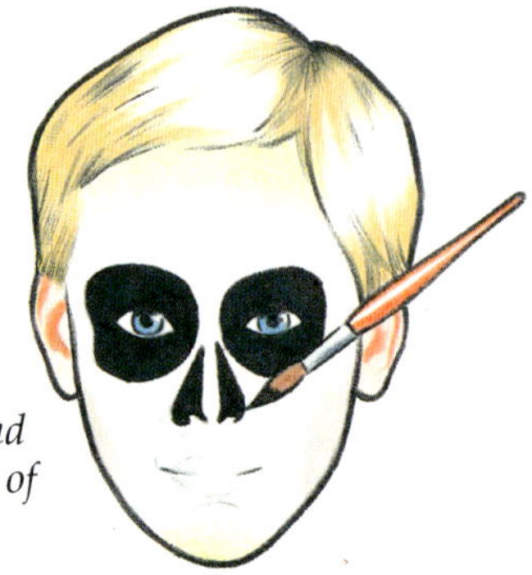

Triangles end around tops of nostrils.

3. Paint two long, black triangles on the end of the nose for the holes where the skull's nose used to be.

Cover hair with black material or a hood to get the total skull effect.

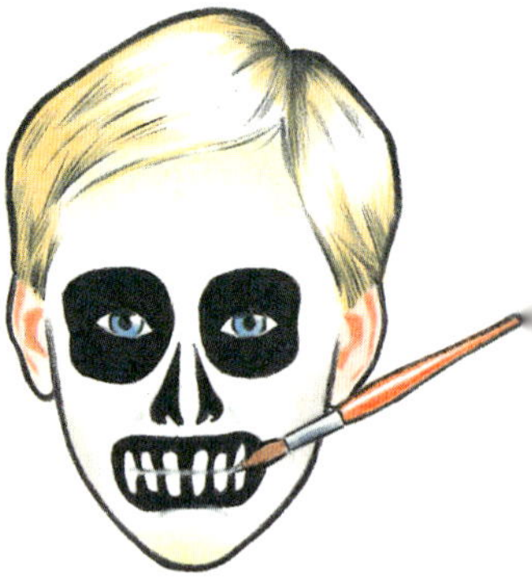

Touch up "teeth" with more white.

4. Outline a big, black oblong around the mouth. Paint black lines across it, leaving white, lumpy "teeth".

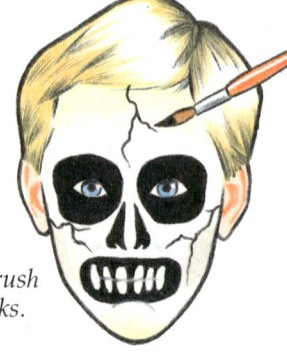

Use a fine brush for thin cracks.

5. Paint jagged, forked cracks in black. If you paint white lines beside them they look as if they are really deep.

Ghoul

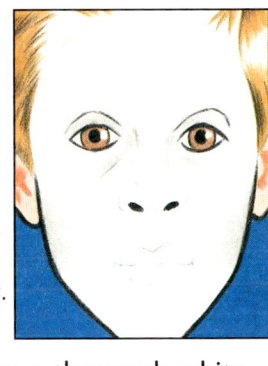

Cover the mouth with white so that it disappears.

1. Sponge a thorough white base. Shade the temples, sides of the nose, cheek hollows and chin in grey.

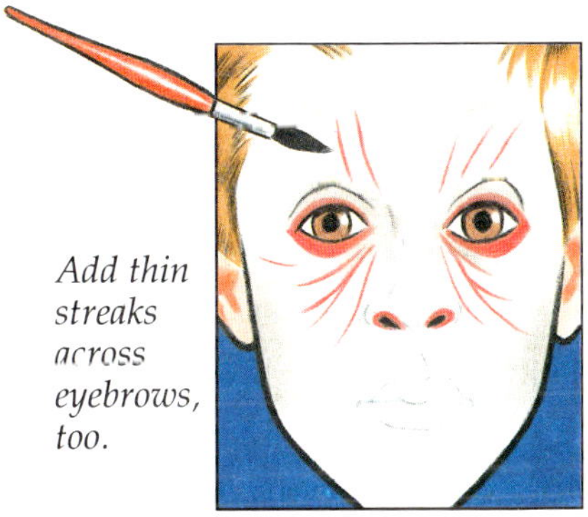

Add thin streaks across eyebrows, too.

2. With pink on a brush, circle the eyes and around the nostrils. Do several thin pink streaks under the eyes.

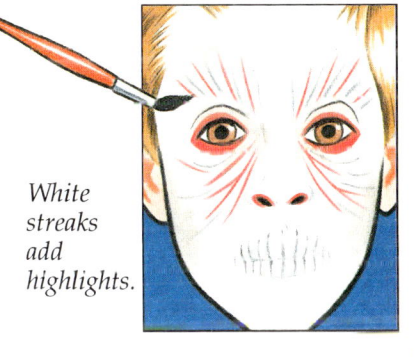

White streaks add highlights.

3. Paint thin, grey wobbly lines across the eyebrows and mouth. Add thin grey lines under the eyes, too.

Skeleton

You can place a whole skeleton on a face, like this. Put a skull on the forehead. Do the arms over the eyebrows. Put the spine and ribs down the nose and the pelvis around the nostrils. Legs go down the creases between nose and mouth. Do the shapes in white, and outline finely in black.

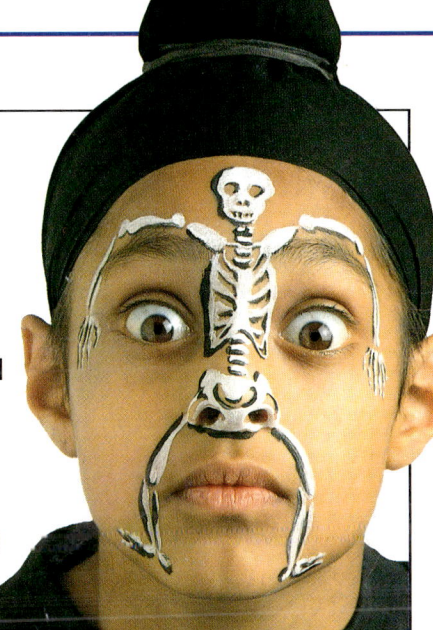

Wrap head and body in a white sheet for the ghostly look.

Monsters

Purple, yellow and dark blue are all good for monster faces. You can see how to do scales and horns here to make them even more frightening.

Scaly reptile

1. For a reptile, sponge yellow from forehead to mouth in a rough "U". Sponge the rest of the face green, blending where they meet.

2. With dark green or black on a thin brush, paint scales like overlapping curved shapes in a triangle up the forehead and cheeks.

3. Do big black ovals around the eyes and over the eyebrows. Do nostrils as for the skull (page 14). Paint a black oblong around the top lip.

4. Paint white fangs down from the corners of the lips. With gold paint, put a forked tongue over the lower lip and onto the chin.

5. When it is dry, fill in the rest of the lower lip with black. Add a dash of dark green or gold inside each of the scales, if you like.

Horns

Horns slope gently out from inner top corner of eye patches.

Dots of red on fangs and in eye-corners make a striking contrast.

How to do horns

Load a brush with white.

Lay the brush, slanting, onto the face. Press down, twist and lift off.

Do the same again, above and a bit to one side of the last one.

Repeat until the horns are long enough. Make the last stroke more upright.

When the strokes are dry, paint dark red, sloping lines between them.

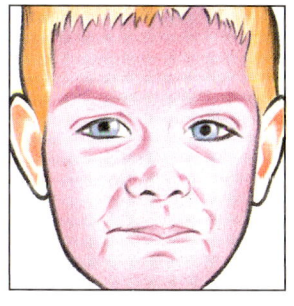

1. Sponge shades of mauve for a two-tone base. Put the darker shade on the forehead, under the cheekbones and around the chin to make hollows.

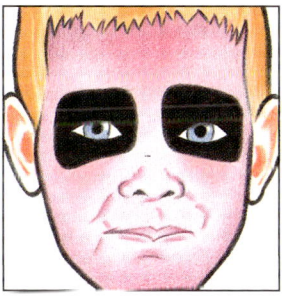

2. Blush the forehead, cheeks and sides of the chin with pink. With black on a brush, paint big, roughly square eye patches.

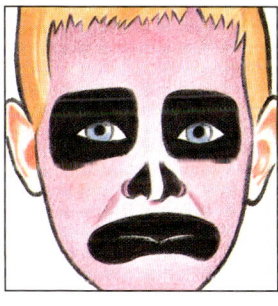

3. Paint a black, downturned clown's mouth (see page 10) with a thick brush. Do black nose-holes as for the skull (see page 14).

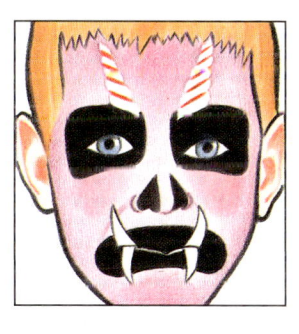

4. When the mouth is completely dry, add white fangs up and down from the corners of the lips. Then add the horns as shown above.

17

Butterflies

How you place a butterfly on a face is very important. Paint the outlines carefully, as shown here, then use your imagination to paint them as brightly as you like. Here are some ideas.

Tip
Both sides of a butterfly should match as nearly as possible. If you do the side you find harder first, it is easier to make the second side match. For right-handed people the left side is usually harder, and the right side is harder if you are left-handed.

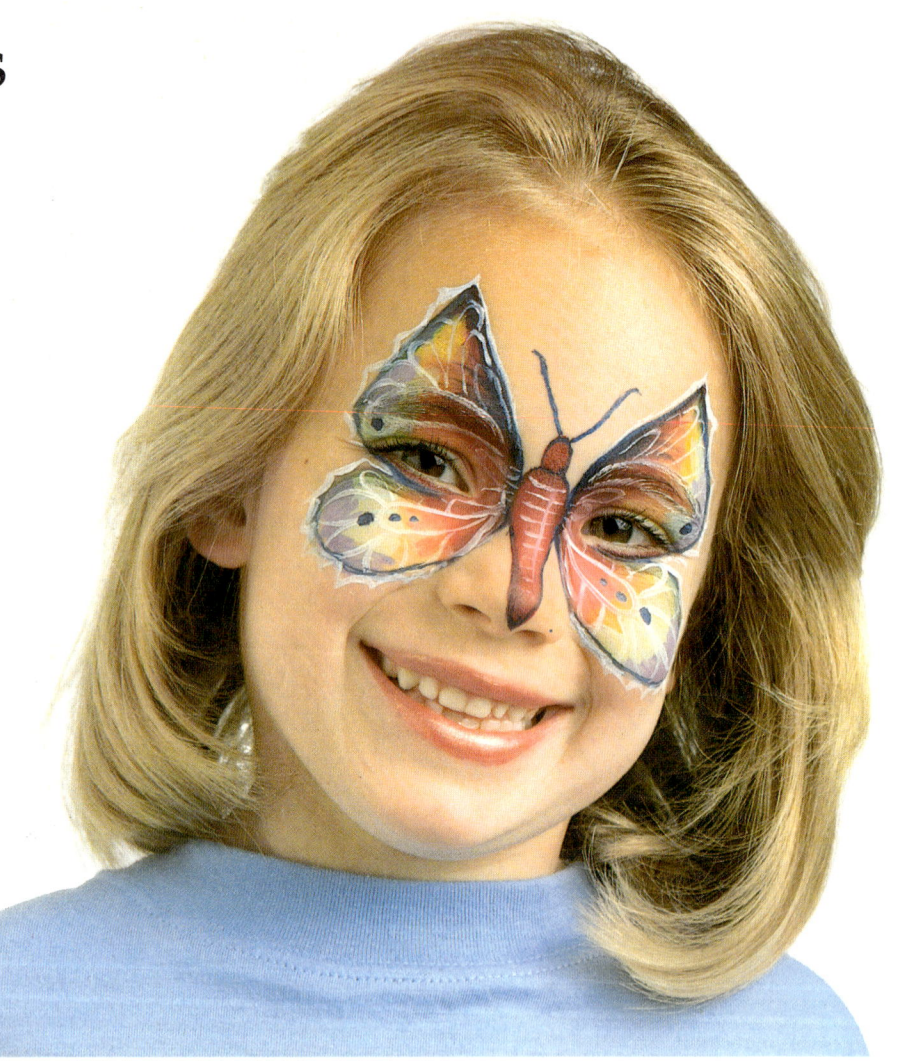

1. With blue on a fine brush, sweep a sloping line up the forehead from the top of the nose. Stop about level with the middle of the eye.

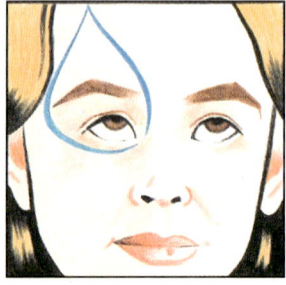

2. Now curve down beside the eye, then underneath it back to where you first started. Ask the model to look up and go close under her eye.

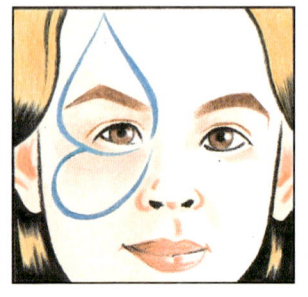

3. Starting in the same place, paint another line that curves around the cheek, about down to the level of the bottom of the ear.

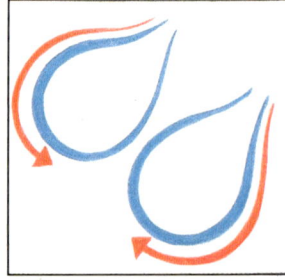

You can do step 3 in two ways: go down beside the nose then around the cheek, or out under the eye first and up by the nose. Try both ways.

Correcting mistakes

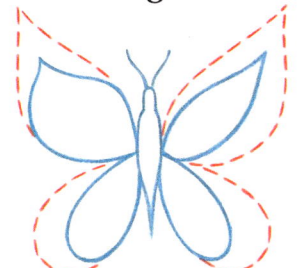

If the shapes don't match, change both until they do (shown by red dotted lines). You can only do it by making them bigger.

To be sure the wings match you must add the "wrong" lines to each, too. They look messy, but will blend in when you paint over them.

More butterflies to try

After step 4, try these other ways to finish the butterfly: just add the body; add the loops and body; do loops, scallops and body. Or just do the outline, loops and scallops on a pretty base.

The butterfly above is done on a pale yellow base with blushed cheeks. The wings are mainly blue to match the model's T-shirt. The scallops are done lightly in black so that they show up nicely.

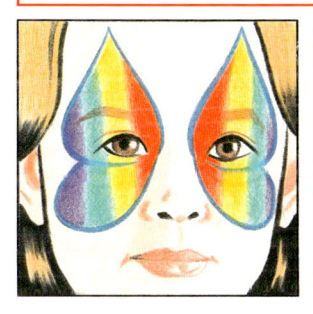

4. Do the other side of the face to match (see above if you go wrong). Fill the shapes in brightly. Paint from the nose out to the edges.

5. With a thin brush and white paint, make a long, smooth loop around each eyebrow. Do another loop in the middle of each bottom wing.

6. With white, make small loops around the big ones. Try not to lift your brush off the face. Then do a scalloped edge all around the wings.

7. Streak a long, red body down the nose (it must join onto the wings at the top). Add a round head, feelers and contrasting stripes.

19

Garlands

These garlands look nicest draped across the forehead and down beside the eyes, curling onto the cheeks. The steps on the right show you the basic way to paint a garland. In the box below you can see how to do some flowers and leaves to put on it.

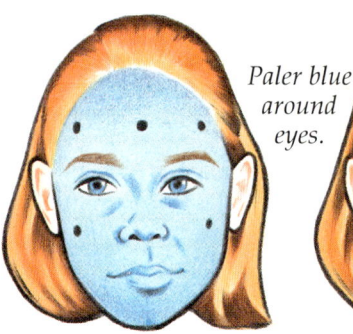

Paler blue around eyes.

1. Sponge a two-tone blue base. Add pink to the forehead, cheeks and chin. Place dots where you want to put the middles of your biggest flowers.

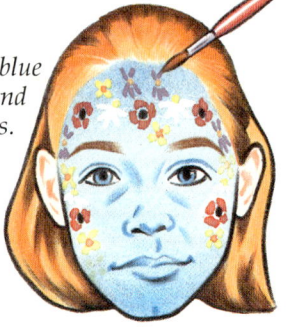

2. Add the big flowers' petals. Now scatter small dots in between, where you will put smaller flowers. Then add their petals, too.

3. It's best to end with a small flower on each cheek. Leaves can link flowers and fill in gaps. Join them with thin, green stems, if you like.

Daisy

Side view

Do a yellow dot. Load a pointed brush with white. Lay it down, pointing at the dot, then lift up for each petal.

Primrose

Do a small orange cross. For double yellow petals, press a brush down, lift up, then press again, a little to one side and over lapping.

Winter wreath

Sponge a pale green base. Shade pink on the forehead, cheeks and chin. Paint a garland of leaves (see below), instead of flowers.

Holly

Paint a gold curve. Add green looping points around it, meeting in a point at each end. Fill in with green. Add red berries with a white dash for "shine".

Mistletoe

Paint two long, oval pale green leaves on a stem. Do two pale yellow berries and add tiny dots to them. Do a dark stripe down the leaves if you like.

Anemone

Do a large black dot. For petals, get red on a thick brush, lay it down beside the dot and move it around a bit to make a blob.

Rose

With a thin brush, paint a pink or red spiral. Lay the brush down and move it around to make three open petals around the edge.

Violet

Do a small yellow dot. Lay down a brush lightly for petals. Do two above and three below (press harder for bigger petals).

Leaves

Lay a brush with green on it down gently. Do leaves in pairs, with one at the end. Their shape depends on the brush (see page 2).

Ivy

Tendrils

Paint a green leaf shape with three points, like this. Do gold lines from the middle out toward each point. Add a few curling tendrils.

Ribbons

Red ribbons and bows make this a **special Christmas wreath**. You could loop red streaks through the wreath and add bows, as shown below, on each cheek.

Do a blob with a loop on each side.

Two ends wiggle down from the blob.

21

Sunset scene

The secret of this face is to blend paint in several strata (bands) across the face. Then add a few simple shapes to suggest your scene. Silhouettes can be very effective. These are outline shapes completely filled in so you recognize what they are by their shape, not by details on them. You can see some silhouettes on the faces shown here.

1. Sponge the whole bottom of the face turquoise from the chin up over the top lip and about level with the bottom of the ears.

Dab to blend the strata together.

You get another shade where strata blend.

2. Working quickly, so the turquoise is still damp, blend yellow on a sponge up over the nose and cheeks and across the eyelids.

Shade cheeks, chin and forehead.

3. Sponge pink over the eyebrows and purple on the forehead. Stripes tend to flatten a face. Give it some shape with purple shading.

Branches curve with the shape of the face.

4. Load a medium brush with black and paint four palm branches. The box on the page opposite shows you how to do them

Palm branches

Start with the tip of the brush, press and make a thick curve, then lift off to make a point.

From the same spot, curve a branch over each brow, one down the nose and one up the forehead.

Add fine, spiky curves from underneath each main curve to make palm fronds (leaves).

Paint branches over nose and forehead.

Black lines for silhouettes of grass on chin.

Do gold lips and crescent moon.

Orange squares look like lit windows in the church.

Snow scene

Blend white, yellow then shades of dark blue up the face. Dab purple on cheeks and forehead. Paint a bare tree and church in black.

Add white for snow on the branches and the church. Do snowflakes with a stipple sponge (see below) or the point of a fine brush.

Stipple sponge

A stipple sponge is made of coarse mesh. You wet it, squeeze it, then rub it in paint and dab gently on the face to make speckles. It's good for snowflakes, stars, a stubbly chin, or a hazy, romantic look on any face. You can buy a stipple sponge from face paint or theatrical suppliers.

Add an island for tree to stand on.

White wavy lines suggest waves.

Do white ripples around fin.

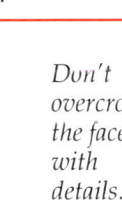

Don't overcrowd the face with details.

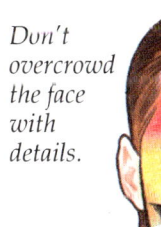

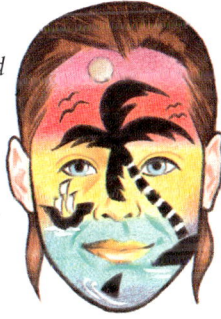

5. Do a line of black blobs with spaces between for the trunk. Each time, press the brush down, then lift. Make them curve onto the cheek.

6. Add more silhouettes, as you like. A curved black triangle on the chin makes a shark's fin; V-shapes in the sky are birds; or try a ship.

7. Streak gold on the joints of the trunk as if they are being caught by the sunlight. Make the face glow with a round gold sun and gold lips.

Designer patterns

You can paint striking faces using shapes and patterns on things you see around you. Look at natural things, such as tree trunks or leaves. Or notice what is behind your model, such as a wallpaper design, and camouflage the face to blend in with it. One idea is to make a face to match her clothes. See how parts of the T-shirt pattern have been used below.

1. Look closely at your model's clothes. Pick out a pattern, or part of one, that you like. Then mix your paints to match.

2. To mix, dab a sponge in one pot, then another and test on the back of your hand; or mix brushfuls of paint on a saucer.

Dots, black wavy lines and orange flower match T-shirt.

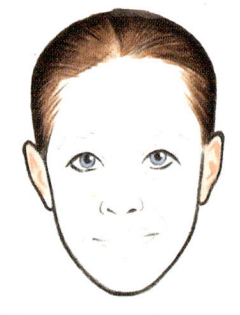

This pattern has a plain white base.

3. Choose a light base shade from the pattern and sponge it on. Do a more interesting two-tone base (paler around the eyes) if you like.

A design like this is a good idea if your model does not know what kind of face she would like painted.

Underline eyes in black so they show up well.

4. Now add the pattern. You do not need to copy exactly, just pick out the strongest or nicest parts. See the opposite page for how to place them.

Placing a pattern

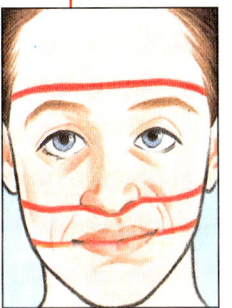

To fit a pattern to a face, place strong lines across on eyebrows, mouth or under the nose.

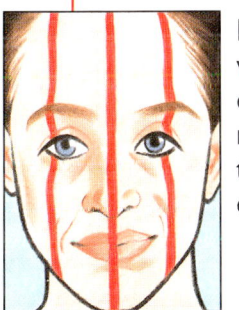

Put strong vertical lines down the nose or down through the eyes.

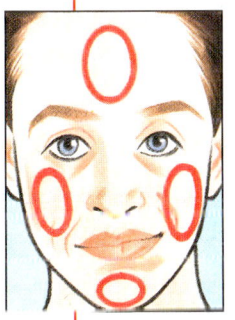

Place main features of the pattern where there is lots of space: on the forehead, cheeks and chin.

Matching

You do not need to copy a pattern to make a face co-ordinate with someone's clothes. Simply paint any of the faces in this book, using shades that go with what they are wearing.

Match-a-bike

This face has been painted to match a green and black racing bike. You can adapt it to match any sports gear.

Sponge two main shades diagonally across the face. With a stipple sponge (page 23), speckle each shade with dots of the other along the join. Add a motif, or symbol. Paint the lips to contrast.

Football crazy

A design like this can show you support a sports' team.

Sponge opposite quarters of the face white. Sponge the other quarters to match the team's gear. When the white is dry, add stripes to match the other quarters with a brush. Straight lines are hard to paint, so do them slowly and carefully.

Graffiti

Writing on a face is fairly tricky. Words with an uneven number of letters work best since you can put the central letter in the middle of the face then add the rest on either side (take great care with spelling - it may help to write the word down on paper first). The best places to write are across the nose or forehead.

25

Robot

Silver and gold paint do not show up very well by themselves on most skins. If you mix them with green, blue or mauve, though, they make a shiny, metallic effect which is great for robots, monsters or aliens.

You could paint gold dots on corners of eye patches.

The dots look like rivets, which are what hold metal sheets together.

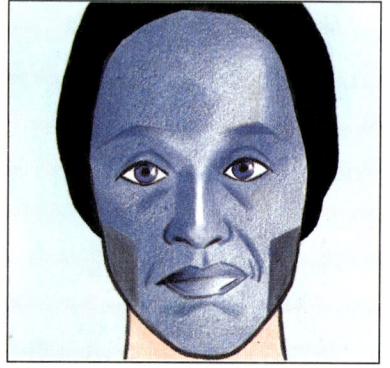

1. Mix deep blue with silver and sponge a base. With dark blue on its own, sponge straight-edged shadows from cheekbones to chin.

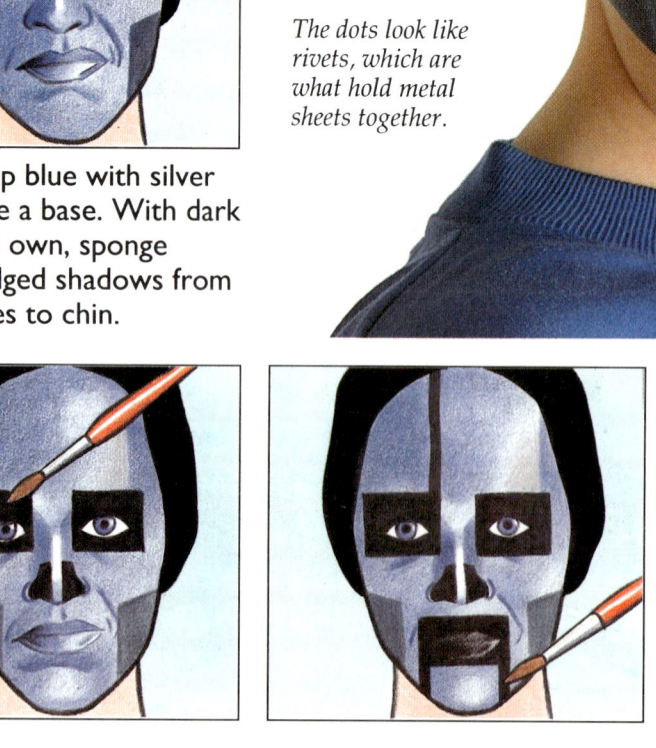

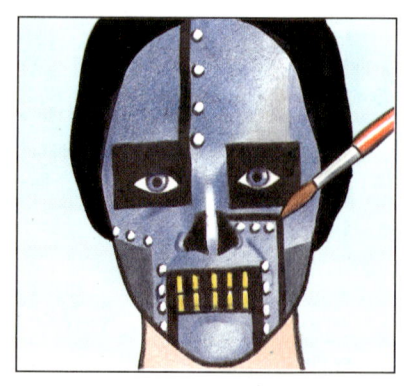

2. With a brush, paint big, black squares around the eyes and fill them in. Do thin black rectangles on the nose above the nostrils.

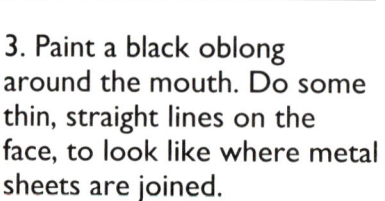

3. Paint a black oblong around the mouth. Do some thin, straight lines on the face, to look like where metal sheets are joined.

4. Place small white dots along the lines. Outline half of each dot in black. Add thin gold lines across the mouth, like a grille.

26

Kabuki

In Japan there is a long tradition of face painting. Kabuki is an ancient form of Japanese drama in which the actors, who are all men, paint their faces in bold, mask-like designs to represent characters. For this Kabuki lion, first sponge a thorough white base.

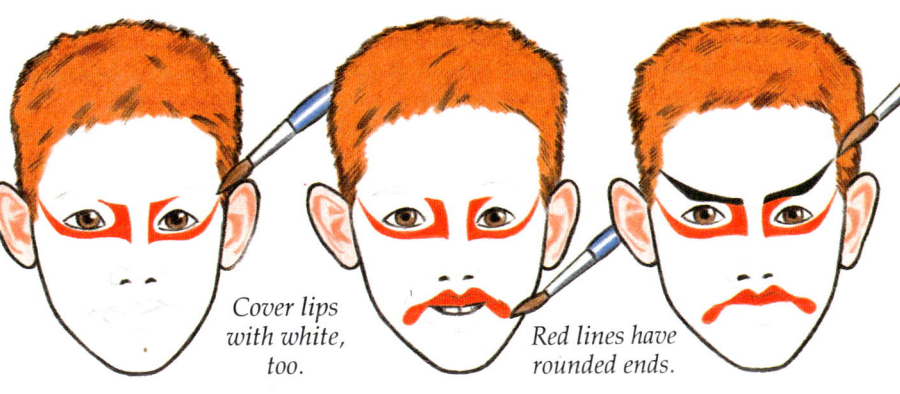

Cover lips with white, too.

Red lines have rounded ends.

1. Paint thick red lines from the inner eyebrows, down the sides of the nose. Then paint out under the eyes and curve up and off to a point.

2. Paint the top lip red and extend each side down onto the chin. Ask the model to keep his lips apart until dry, so the red does not smudge.

3. Do thick, black eyebrows. Press on your brush and sweep out along the brow. Lift off and curve up to a point at the outer edge.

Red, white, black

The Kabuki face above uses only red, white and black paint. Here are some more you can try.

Always do a thorough white base first, then add the red details, then the black ones.

There are lots of other faces in this book you can do using only red, white and black (mix them to make pink and grey, too): see mouse (page 4), spotted dog (page 6), vampire (page 13), skull (page 14), and ghoul (page 15), for example.

Sponge red on hair, if you like.

Owl

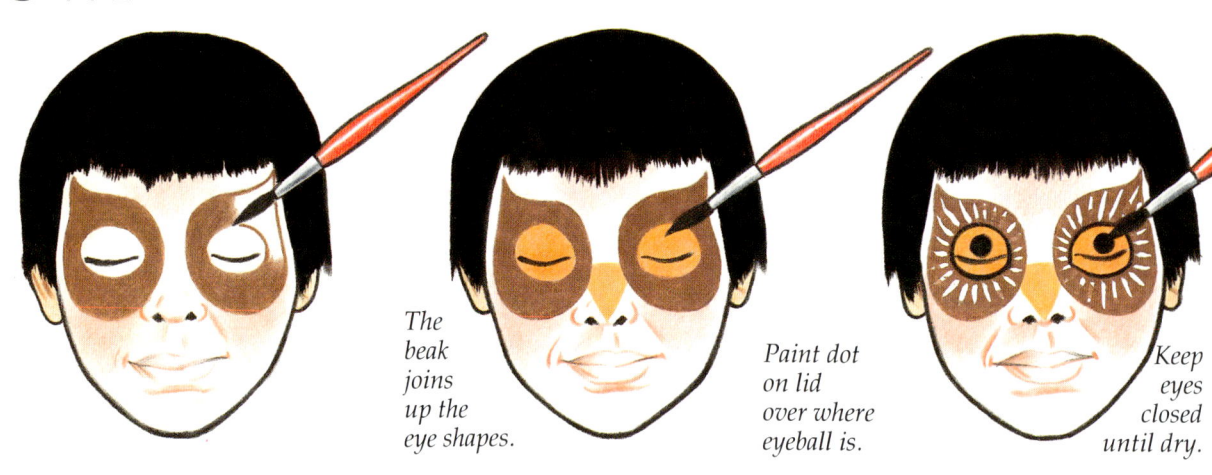

The beak joins up the eye shapes.

Paint dot on lid over where eyeball is.

Keep eyes closed until dry.

1. With brown on a brush, paint an owl's face shape around the eyes. Fill it in except for a circle on the lid and just under the eye.

2. Paint a yellow triangle for a beak on the nose. Put orange in the circles you left unpainted on the eyelids and under the eyes.

3. When the brown is dry, do white streaks out all around the eyes. With black, outline the orange circles and put a dot in each.

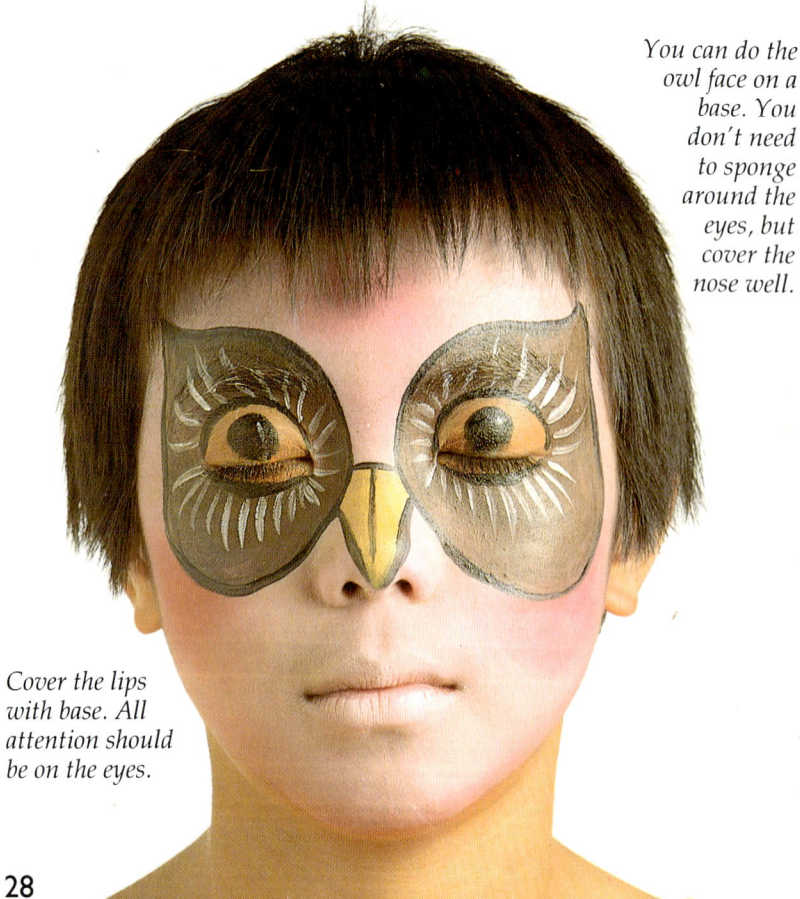

You can do the owl face on a base. You don't need to sponge around the eyes, but cover the nose well.

Cover the lips with base. All attention should be on the eyes.

Add black streak down middle of beak.

When the model closes his eyes, the owl opens his.

4. Outline the whole shape in black to tidy up the edges. When the black eye spot is very dry, add a white blob for a gleam of light.

Bat

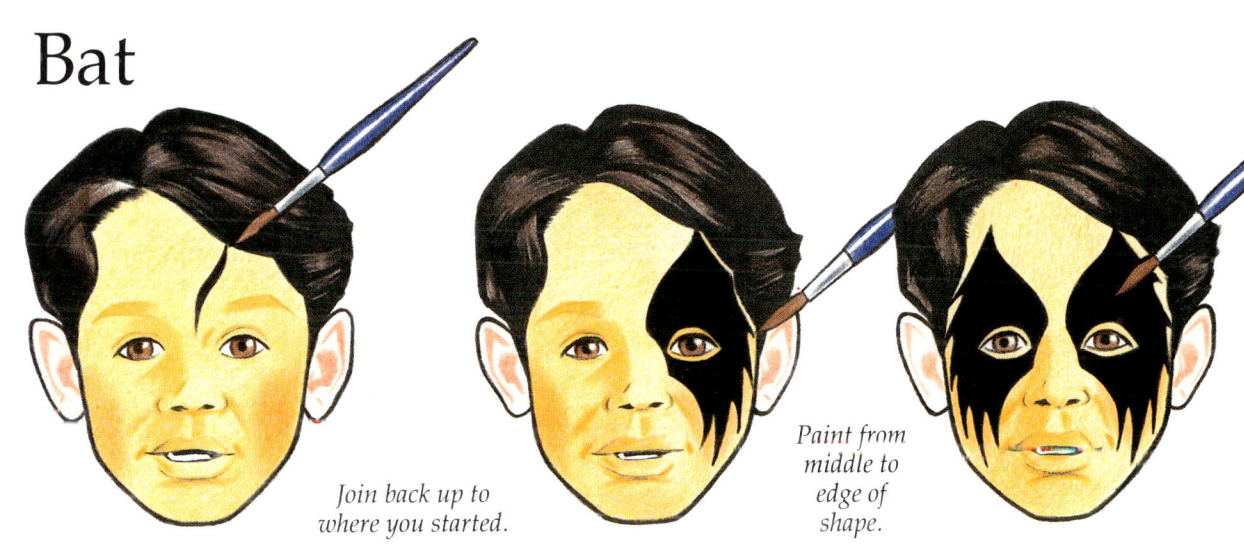

1. Sponge a yellow base. With black on a brush, slant a line up the forehead from the top of the nose to make a big point above the eye.

Join back up to where you started.

2. Do looping points down the side of the face and two long points down to about mouth level. Curve back up to the top of the nose.

Paint from middle to edge of shape.

3. Do the other side to match. Outline a circle around the eye sockets and just under the eyes. Fill the rest in with black.

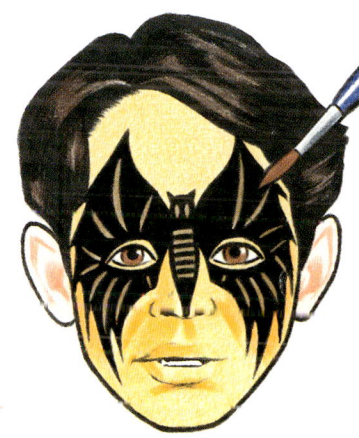

Do the outline on the side you find hardest first (see page 18).

Add gold eyes and streaks across body.

Two or three lines fork from same place.

Do gold details on the black, when it is very dry.

Paint lips black to complete the face.

4. Do a head and long body down the nose. Underline the eyes in gold. Make gold veins fork out from near the eyes to each point.

Party pieces

You can use your face painting skills to have fun at parties. You and your friends could paint your best faces on each other, or try doing faces all on the same subject to make a theme: you could do a tiger (page 9), some clowns (pages 10-11) and the strongman, lion and seal from these two pages for a circus theme, for example. You could take photographs to keep as a record.

Here are some more faces to inspire you. Some are variations on ideas from earlier in the book and some are for special occasions.

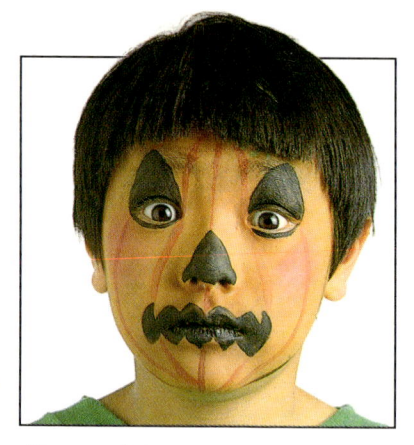

Pumpkin

Do an orange base. Paint red curved stripes down the face that meet at the chin. Do black triangles over the eyes and on the end of the nose, and a black zig-zag mouth to make a carved pumpkin.

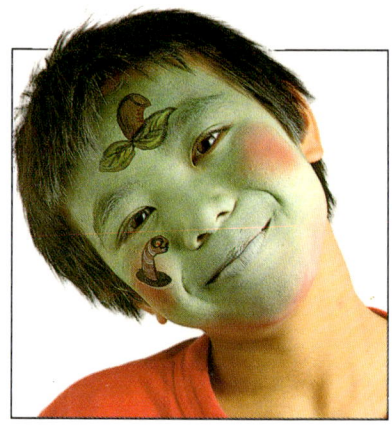

Apple

Do a halloween apple with a green base and pink cheeks; put leaves and a stem on the forehead. Paint half a worm on the cheek, with a black circle across the end to look like a hole in the apple.

Strongman

Do a white base and blush pink cheeks; add thick, black curly eyebrows and a line under each eye; paint a black, twirly moustache and red lips. He could also be the circus ringmaster.

Lion

Do a cat face (see pages 8-9) with a yellow-brown base and white, sponged muzzle. Lions have a beard so sponge the chin white, too. Try to make the hair stick out like a lion's mane if you can.

Seal

Do a seal with a white base and mauve shading. Add grey eye patches and a muzzle. It has black whiskers, nose and lips. Can the model make a seal noise and slap his arms together like flippers?

Angel

Sponge a sky blue base and blush the cheeks. Stipple (page 23) white stars. Paint wings across the eyebrows, a robe down the nose, and arms on the cheeks. Add a head and halo.

Christmas tree

Sponge a white base. Paint a green fir tree down the nose. The branches spread onto the cheeks. Do a brown trunk from the nose to top lip and add decorations as you like. Paint red lips.

Iceman

Sponge a mid-blue base, leaving a mask shape around the eyes. When the blue is dry, paint the mask shape white. Do thin, white icicles all around the edge of the mask. Add white stars.

Japanese doll

On a white base, sponge a pink band from brows to nose tip. Do a white line down the nose. Outline the eyes in black, making a point at the side. Slope black brows up. Do a small, red mouth.

Valentine

Paint a special garland (see page 20) for Valentine's or Mothers' Day. Do a white base and pink cheeks; add hearts and ribbons. Can you think what to do for a Fathers' Day face?

Grey rabbit

Here's another version of the rabbit on page 5, with a grey base instead of purple. You could do the same face on everyone at a party, but paint each one to match the person's clothes.

Portrait gallery

Here are photographs of all the children who had their faces painted for this book. At the bottom of this page it tells you which pages you can see them on. Have a look at the photographs, then see how different some of them look in their face paint; or try to guess which faces they modelled before you look at the list.

1. Henry Swallow: p17. **2.** Jonny Greensted: tiger p9. **3.** Sam Greensted: p7. **4.** Amelia McKilveney: p6. **5.** Lucy Palmer: leopard p9. **6.** Rupert Palmer: p8. **7.** Christopher Sweeney: vampire p13. **8.** William White: p16. **9.** Sukhbir Rihal: skeleton p15. **10.** Alice Skidmore: p24,26. **11.** Lydia Childs: p21,22, Christmas tree p30. **12.** Alastair Baird: p14. **13.** Aimée Baird: p18. **14.** Caroline Radway: p12, bike p25, lion p30. **15.** Mary Caudron: p19, Valentine p31. **16.** Daisy Caudron: p23. **17.** Stefanie Fuller: hag p13, angel p30. **18.** Damion Fuller: iceman p31. **19.** Oliver Pugh: p29, seal p31. **20.** Sam Jenkins: graffiti p25, strongman p30. **21.** John Lau: p28, apple p31. **22.** Chun Lau: pumpkin p31. **23.** Alex Jones: football p25. **24.** Rachel Mylon: Japanese doll p30. **25.** Wesley West: p15. **26.** Damian Phillips: p27. **27.** Oliver Wiffen: p10. **28.** Jemima Bokaie: p11. **29.** Kate Lewis: p20. **30.** Karen Divall: rabbit p31. **31.** Francesca Tyler: p4. **32.** Hannah Kirby-Jones p5.

32   To find face paint suppliers, look in your yellow pages telephone directory under **Fancy dress**. Ring and ask if they supply water-based face paint. Some makes to ask for are Grimas (U.K.), Mehron's and Stein's (U.S.A.).

MASKS

Ray Gibson

With thanks to Noorece Ahmed, Eliza Borton, Joanna Borton, Jessica Borton, Rebecca Treays, Maria Wheatley and Marie-Lou Cousin.

Contents

Making masks	34	Tiger	46
Skeleton and Frankenstein	36	Wolf	48
Hovering bees	38	Bright bird	50
Octopus and Clown	40	Goggle-eyed monster	52
Fiery dragon	42	Dracula	54
Detective and Movie star	44	Templates	56

Making masks

Before you start, it is a good idea to gather everything you need. The photograph on the right shows you the basic materials and equipment for mask-making, while the special things you need are listed in the introduction to each mask.

You can find PVA glue* and paper reinforcement rings in stationers' or office supply stores. If you don't have tracing paper you can use greaseproof paper, while some food packaging provides a good supply of thin cardboard.

*You can buy hat and shirring elastic** in dressmakers' stores.*

Fastening your mask

There are three different ways of fastening your mask, depending on its shape, and whether it is heavy or light.

Hat elastic

Hat elastic is thin, but very strong and is good for fastening heavy masks. You need a piece about 25cm (10in) long to fasten one mask. See right for how best to attach this elastic.

1. Poke small holes with a pencil. Do this 1cm (½in) from the sides and level with the eyeholes.

2. On the inside of the mask, stick paper reinforcement rings over the holes. This prevents any tears.

3. Thread the elastic through both holes and knot the ends at the edges. Tape down the loose ends.

Shirring elastic

This fine elastic is good for lighter masks. These masks have slits in the sides for you to wind the elastic through. You will need about 25cm (10in) for each mask.

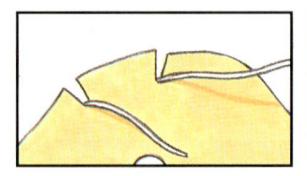

1. Slide the elastic, either side, through the top slit and around to the bottom. Leave a tail.

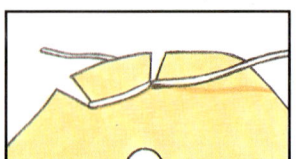

2. Pull each short end up through the top slit and around the front. Pull firmly through the bottom slit.

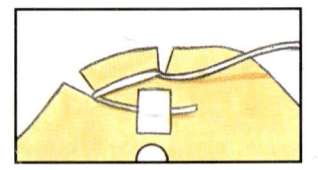

3. Make sure the elastic fits around your head snugly. Then tape down the loose end on either side.

34

* Household glue (U.S) ** Elastic cord and elastic thread (U.S)

Cardboard strips

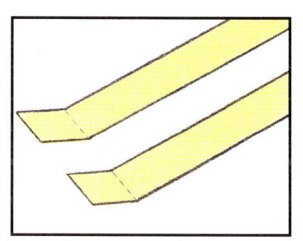

1. Cut two pieces of thin cardboard 30 x 3cm (12 x 1½in). Fold up 2cm (1in) tabs at one end of each.

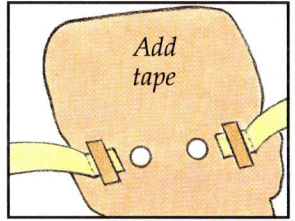

2. Stick the tabs, using PVA glue, to the back of the mask, 3cm (1½in) away from the eyeholes.

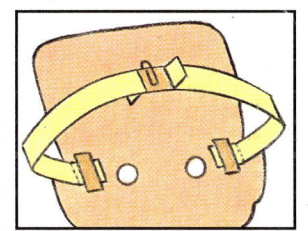

3. Wrap the strips around your head. Add a paper clip to hold the headband together until you tape it.

Cutting eyeholes

Poke the point of a sharp pencil in the middle of the eyehole. Push the blade of your scissors into the hole. Make small snips to the edge before cutting the circle out.

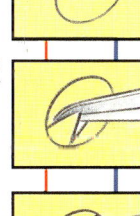

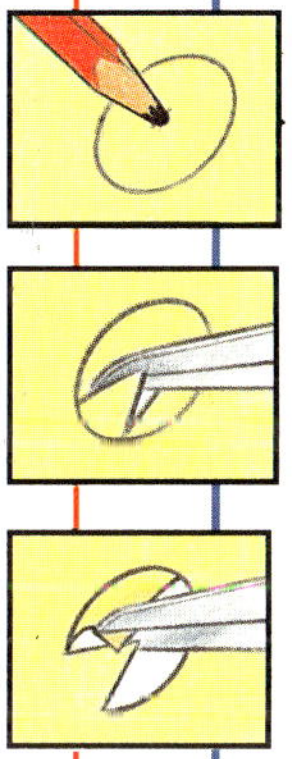

Tracing templates

1. Lay a sheet of tracing paper over the template. Slide on a few paper clips.

2. With a pencil, carefully trace all the lines and any special markings.

3. Turn the tracing over and draw thickly with a soft pencil over the outlines.

4. Turn the tracing back over and lay onto paper or cardboard. Pencil over the lines.

The shape will appear.

Tracing half-templates

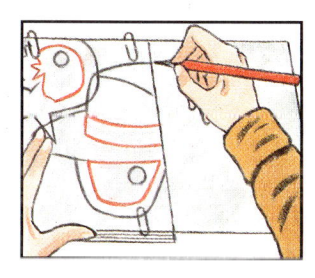

1. Fold a sheet of tracing paper. Open it out and lay the fold on the template's edge.

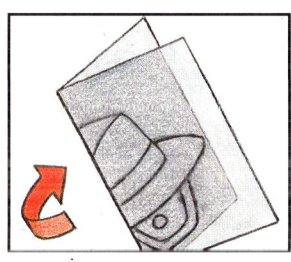

2. Trace the shape. Take off the tracing and fold it. The lines will show through.

3. Carefully copy the outline showing through. This will complete the shape.

4. Now open out the tracing to see your template. Then follow steps 3-4 above.

35

Skull

The secret of this creepy mask is to paint it with tea or coffee to make it look really old and decayed. First copy the template on page 63 onto white thin cardboard. You will also need: strong black tea or coffee; shirring elastic and some paints.

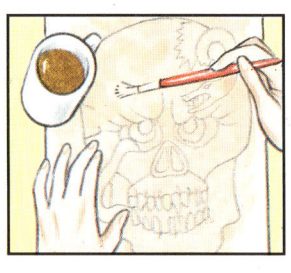

1. Paint over the skull with cold tea or coffee. It's good to leave some blobs and blotches. Now let it dry completely.

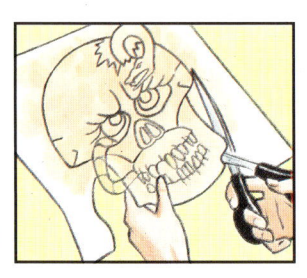

2. Go over all the pencil lines in black. Cut out the mask. Snip out the eyeholes and attach the elastic (see pages 34-35).

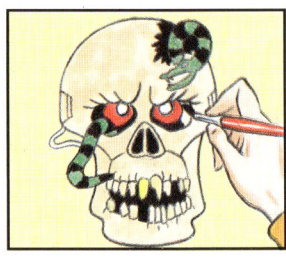

3. Now paint your mask as shown on the photograph. Try different shades of grey, dirty yellow and brown for the teeth.

Tip

Make these two masks look more lifelike by cutting the lower part of the nose.

Stick the scissor point just below the top of the nose and then carefully cut around.

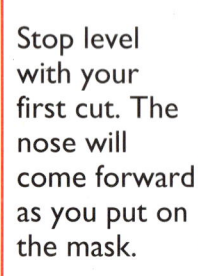

Stop level with your first cut. The nose will come forward as you put on the mask.

Frankenstein

Everyone will recognize this gruesome monster from films and books. The mask is very dramatic especially if you wear black. Copy the template on page 62 onto white thin cardboard. You also need red, black and brown paints, and more thin cardboard.

1. Carefully cut out the mask. Snip the eyeholes (see page 35). Now go over all the pencil lines with a black felt-tip pen.

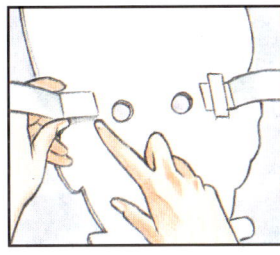

2. Cut two strips of cardboard 30 x 3cm (12 x 1½in). Fold back 2cm (1in) for tabs and glue on. Add tape to hold (see page 35).

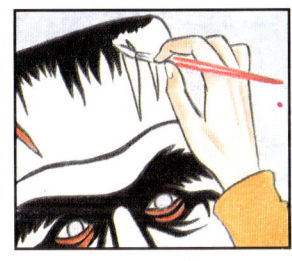

3. Paint the mask as shown on the photograph. When the mask is dry, wrap the strips around your head and tape.

Tip

To give Frankenstein even more character, dab on a little shading. Do this by dipping cotton wool* into some runny dark paint. Wipe the cotton wool* along some spare paper to sop up most of the paint. Then, when almost dry, dab under the eyes and around the mouth. This will give you a subtle shading effect.

*cotton ball (U.S.)

Hovering bees

For this eye-catching mask, first trace the basic mask template on page 60 onto thin cardboard and then cut it out. To decorate it, you need some bright flowery wrapping paper, 12 thin silver florists' wires*, white paper, shirring elastic, and yellow paper 24 x 3cm (9½ x 1½in).

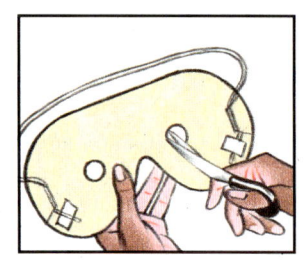

1. Take your mask and snip the lines at the sides. Attach elastic and cut out eyeholes as described on pages 34-35.

2. Cut out flowers and leaves from the wrapping paper. Glue them onto the mask to cover it completely, as shown below.

3. Cut the wires to lengths of 10 to 15 cm (4 to 6in). Bend the ends of each and tape to the back of the mask, like this.

The bees on this mask will move and hover as you walk around.

Lightly bend the wires, some forwards and some back.

Arranging the flowers

Start at the edge of the mask. Make the first flowers and leaves stick out over the edge.

Move towards the middle of the mask. Glue the flowers on overlapping. Use fewer leaves.

Don't worry if flowers cover the eyeholes. Cut them out again from the back when the glue is dry.

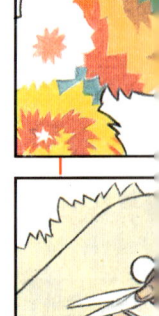

38

* You can buy these easily and cheaply in your local florists'.

Draw the lines lengthways.

The thick stripe is at the front end.

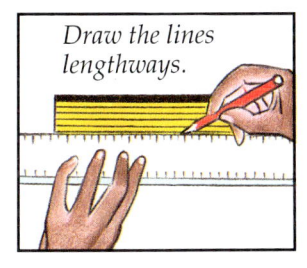

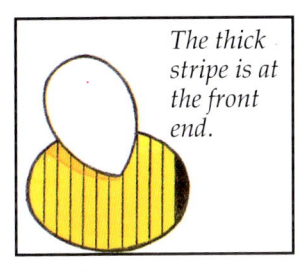

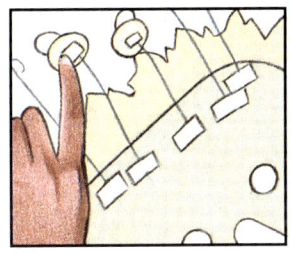

4. For the bees, draw black lines across the yellow paper with a ruler and a felt-tip pen. Do a really thick line at the top.

5. Cut the paper into twelve 2cm (½in) pieces. Now round off the corners of each piece to make fat bee shapes.

6. Cut out 12 white teardrop shapes from white paper. Glue one onto each bee, slant them slightly away from the front end.

7. Turn over the mask so it is right side down. Slip a bee face down behind the tip of each wire and tape it on.

You can add some glitter to the silver paper.

Give the fish glittery eyes.

Leaping fish

Prepare the same basic mask as before. Use blue cardboard, or paint it. Glue on wavy strips of green and silver paper.

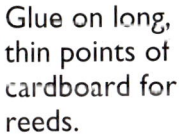

Glue on long, thin points of cardboard for reeds.

Tape wires on (step 3, opposite) and tape fish shapes to their tips.

39

Octopus

These jolly carnival masks cover your whole head and are very simple to make. For the octopus, cut a piece of vinyl wallpaper 100cm (40in) long and another piece 75cm (30in) long. You will also need green and orange thick paint, a sponge, a stapler and some paper clips.

Plain sides if patterned wallpaper.

Use paper clips to hold.

Move paper clips to sides.

1. Dab the wallpaper with a sponge dipped in green paint. Let it dry, then wipe with a damp sponge to get a pale watery look.

2. Fold the short edges of the larger piece of paper. Use paper clips to hold the ends together. Draw a large octopus head.

3. Carefully cut out the shape, moving the paper clips to the sides. Now staple the edges, leaving the bottom open.

You can draw a black line around the eyes.

Tentacles

Fold the smaller piece of paper in half lengthways. Do this two more times. Now open it out and cut along the fold lines to make eight strips. Cut one end of each into a rounded point.

4. Put the mask on and ask a friend to help you mark places for the eyeholes*. Take off the mask and cut out the eyeholes.

Slant outer tentacles.

5. Paint large orange eyes around the eyeholes. Staple four tentacles onto the back and four onto the front (see left).

*Take care not to hurt your eyes.

Clown

This clown is made in much the same way as the octopus. Cut a piece of wallpaper 100cm (40in) long and fold the short edges. Draw a clown's head and then cut it out (see steps 2-3 on page 40). You will also need some bright crêpe paper and a piece of cardboard.

Any pattern goes on the inside.

1. Cut long crêpe paper strips 6cm (2½in) wide. Pleat and staple them around the edge of one head shape.

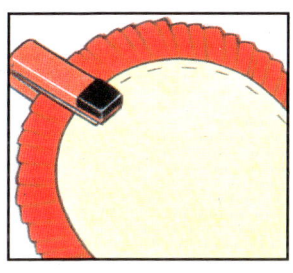

2. Place the other head shape on top of the frilled half and staple the edges together. Keep the plain side up.

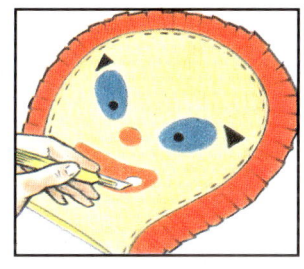

3. Cut eyeholes (see step 4 on page 40) and then paint on a mouth around them. Add a nose, eyes and eyebrows.

You can use glitter pen to outline eyes, mouth and nose.

4. Cut a piece of stiff cardboard about 12 x 7cm (5 x 3in) and glue, as shown, to the inside bottom edge of the mask.

5. Tie a huge bow out of crêpe paper. Now glue it to the cardboard that is hanging down at the front of the mask.

41

Fiery dragon

To make this ferocious-looking mask you need: thin red cardboard; orange crêpe paper; yellow, white and black paint; green glitter (if you like) and shirring elastic.

Although it is so dramatic, this mask is quick and easy to make. Trace and cut out the shape in thin cardboard using the template on page 64. Go over the cutting lines on the face in blue. This makes it easier to see where to cut.

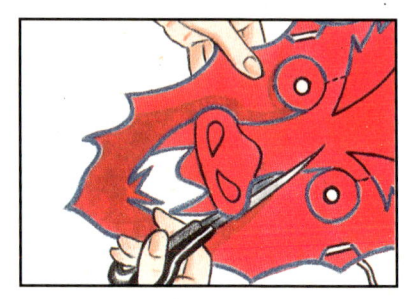

1. Snip out the eyeholes and attach the elastic (see pages 34-35). Cut along all the blue lines. See the tip box for cutting hints. Paint the face.

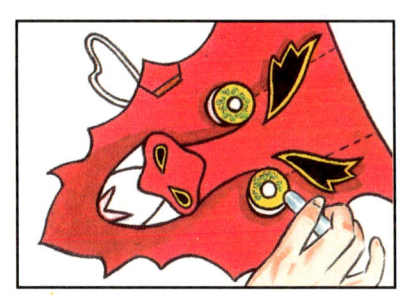

2. When the paint is dry, go around all the features in black. Dab a little glue around the eyes and scatter on green glitter, if you like.

Cutting the mask

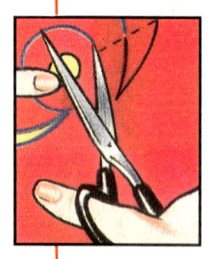

Cut along the blue lines. Poke a hole with the point of your scissors to start off.

Fold along the dotted lines and pinch the cardboard back. This helps the features to pop out.

The nose, brows and eyes come forward to make the mask look really dramatic.

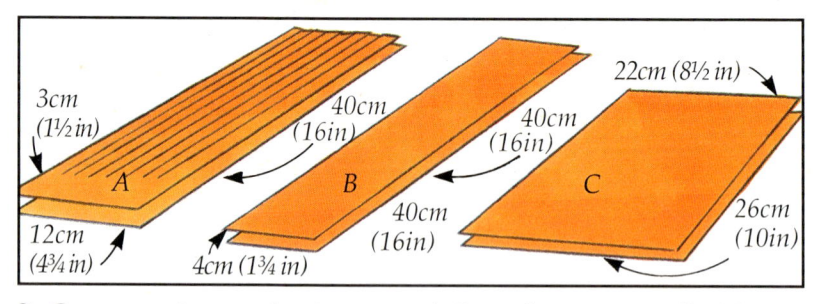

3. Cut two pieces of crêpe paper to each of the sizes shown above. Snip along the pieces called A up to 3cm (1½in) from the end.

A: 3cm (1½in) × 12cm (4¾in)
B: 40cm (16in) × 4cm (1¾in)
C: 22cm (8½in) × 26cm (10in), 40cm (16in)

4. Snip the pieces called B up to 2cm (1in) from the end; and then snip the pieces called C up to 9cm (3½in) from the end.

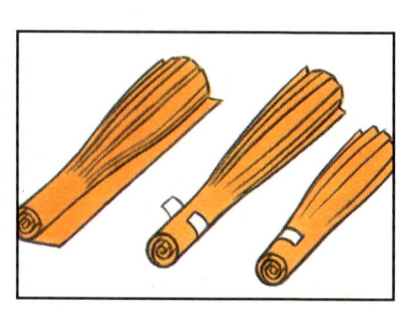

5. Tightly roll up each strip at the short uncut end and stick tape over the join to hold together. Use two shades of crêpe paper, if you like.

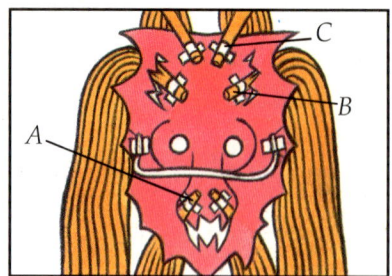

6. Tape pieces A behind the nostrils; pieces B behind the brows; pieces C at the top of the mask. Then tease the tassels around the mask.

You can add foil to eyes and add extra markings to give more expression. Tape on extra tassels if you like.

Detective

Before you start this mask, cut out a basic mask shape from thin cardboard using the template on page 60, and set aside. You will also need: thin cardboard; piece of black plastic; black paint; a thick black felt-tip pen and hat elastic. You can attach this the same way as shirring elastic if you like (see page 34).

1. Copy the template on page 61 onto thin cardboard. Go over the lines in black (keep the tracing to use later).

2. Cut around the shape and snip out the eyeholes. Paint the hatband and frame of the glasses with black paint.

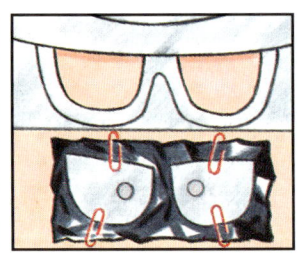

3. Cut out the lenses of the glasses from your tracing and lay them onto a piece of black plastic. Use paper clips to hold.

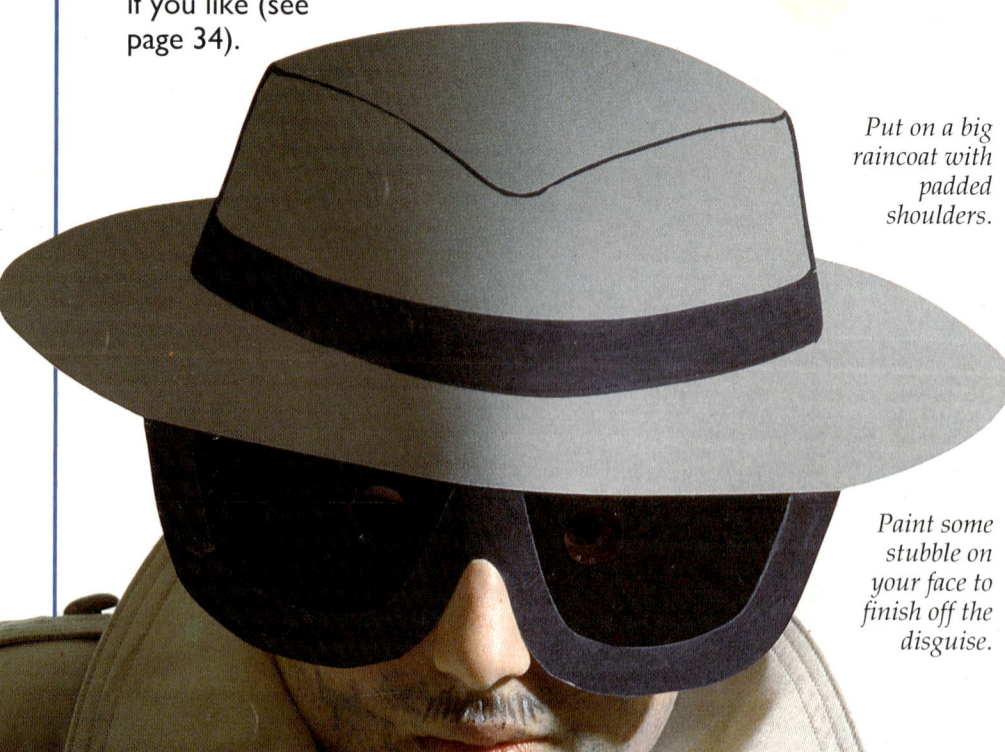

Put on a big raincoat with padded shoulders.

4. Cut around the pieces. Then snip out the eyeholes; bend the pieces back to make the job easier. Glue the lenses onto the mask.

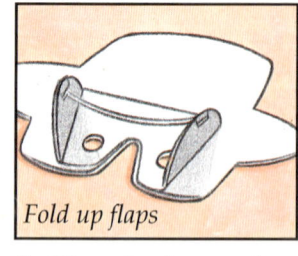

Paint some stubble on your face to finish off the disguise.

Fold up flaps

5. Glue the front of the basic mask to the back of the main mask. Attach elastic to the flaps.

Movie star

This glamorous mask is great fun for when you want to dress up. Make it in the same way as the detective. First cut out a basic mask out of thin cardboard using the template on page 60. You will also need kitchen foil, thin cardboard and a glitter pen to decorate the mask.

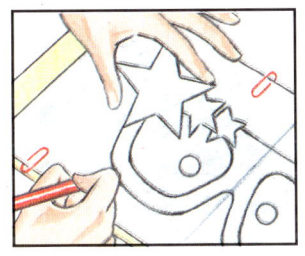

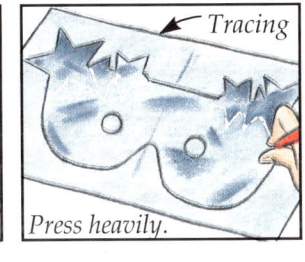

1. Trace and copy the template on page 61 onto a piece of thin cardboard. Keep the tracing as you will need it later.

Smooth down.

2. Carefully cut out the shape. Spread glue over the front of the mask then lay it face down onto a piece of foil.

Tracing

Press heavily.

3. Turn over the mask and trim the edges and eyeholes. Lay the tracing over the top and pencil over the stars so they stand out.

Add more glitter to the mask for a really sparkly effect.

4. See steps 3-5 opposite for how to stick on the black plastic lenses, and how to attach the basic mask with elastic.

5. Go around all the edges and points of the stars with glitter pen.

Tiger

Use the templates on pages 56-57 to copy the shape of this fierce tiger. You can make other animals from the big cat family, such as a panther, leopard or lion, using the same templates. To make the tiger you will need orange stiff paper; thin white cardboard to make whiskers; black, white, yellow and red paints. Use the photograph as a guide for painting the mask.

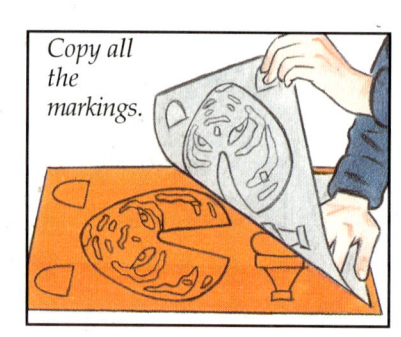

Copy all the markings.

1. Cut out all the shapes copied from the template. Snip out the eyeholes (see pages 34-35 for help on doing all this).

Use paper clips to hold until dry.

2. Take the ears and turn one over to make a left and right ear. Bend the inner corner of each and glue down. Let them dry.

Mix red and white paints for the pink nose.

Painting the eyes

Use a thin paintbrush. Paint the iris yellow and then let it dry.

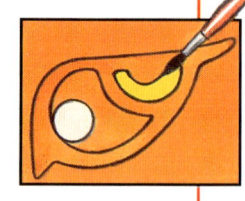

Add the black outline and paint in the pupil.

Paint white around the eyeholes.

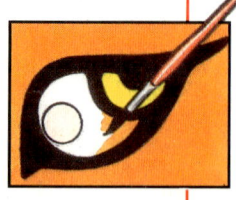

You could add white highlights to the pupil.

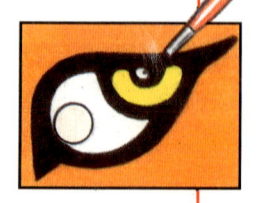

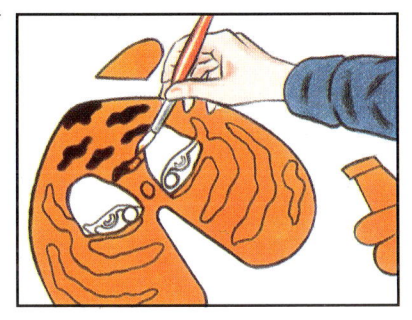

3. Paint the pieces; you can use the photograph as a guide. Outline the features in black. Look at the box on the left for help painting the eyes.

Cut out and stick on long black or white whiskers.

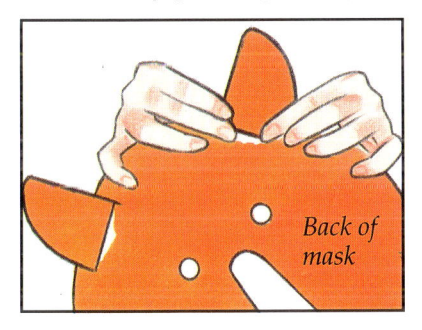

Back of mask

4. Glue the ears behind the face, between the marks at the top. Place the ears so that the folded sides face each other. Let the glue dry.

Panther

Use black paper. Glue on a piece of black plastic to make a shiny nose. Paint the iris bright yellow and add light brown around the eyeholes. Paint the mouth red and the teeth white. Cut six small tapering strips out of black paper and glue them, three each side, pointing up just above the eyes.

Leopard

Use light brown paper and paint on black spots. Paint the eyes yellowish-green.

Lion

Use brown paper. Before adding the headband, glue the mask onto a large piece of brown paper and draw and cut out a shaggy mane. Paint the eyes yellow.

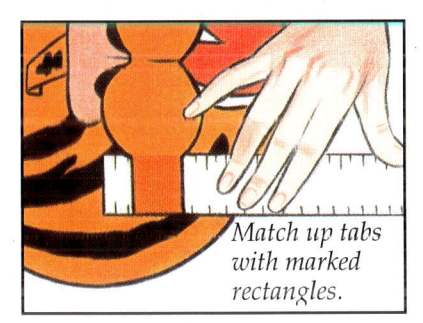

Match up tabs with marked rectangles.

5. Fold down all the tabs on the muzzle and glue them onto the face. Press the tabs down with the end of a ruler so you don't squash the shape.

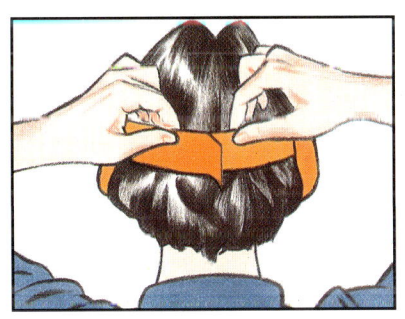

6. Make a headband out of strips of orange paper (see page 35 for how to do this). Make sure it fits your head snugly before you tape it.

Whiskers

Cut long, thin pointed whiskers in different lengths from white cardboard.

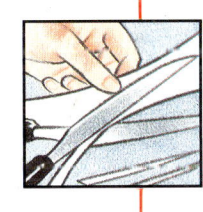

Glue the unpointed ends onto the muzzle. Paint on black dots as shown.

47

Wolf

To make this wolf mask, copy and cut out the templates on pages 58-59. You need: a large sheet of dark grey stiff paper; light grey stiff paper 16 x 16cm (6½ x 6½in); a piece of thin white cardboard; toilet tissue; a spongy cleaning cloth and some black plastic for the nose.

1. Cut out the eyeholes (see page 35 for how to do this), then copy the photograph to paint the eyes. Let it dry.

Add paper clips until dry.

2. Make the headband (see below). Turn over one ear to make a left and right ear. Bend the inner corners in and glue.

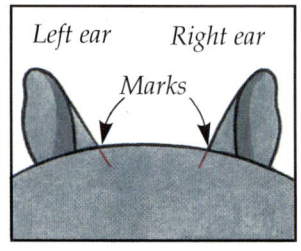

Left ear   Right ear   Marks

3. When dry, glue the ears behind the mask. Line them up with the marks. Make sure you put them on the correct sides.

Headband

Cut two strips of dark grey paper 30 x 3cm (12 x 1½in). Fold back 2cm (1in) on each as tabs.

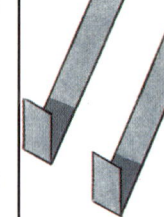

Glue the tabs to the back of the mask, with the edges level with the eyes and 3cm (1½in) away.

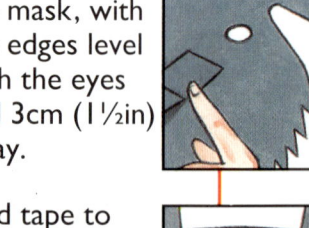

Add tape to hold. To fit, overlap bands around your head. Paper clip together, then tape.

48

All edges meet.

4. Take the muzzle. Bend the fold lines down. Glue the front pieces together on top of each other for the muzzle shape.

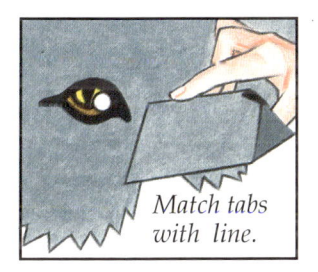

Match tabs with line.

5. Glue the tabs on the muzzle and stick it onto the face. Glue the teeth onto the inside of the muzzle, at the front.

Brown bear

Cut out the templates on pages 58-59 using brown paper. Make the mask in the same way as the wolf. Paint the inner ears.

Stick both corners of the ears down 1cm (½in) before gluing. Stick on beige or cream eyebrows, but don't paint eyes.

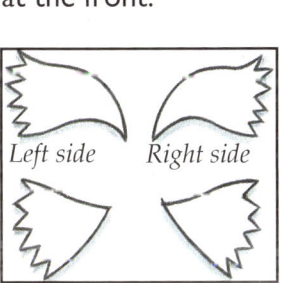

Left side   Right side

6. Take the brow and cheek pieces and lay them out, as shown. Cut four small squares of sponge cleaning cloth.

7. Glue a square of sponge cloth to the back of all the pieces to make them stand out from the face. Stick them on.

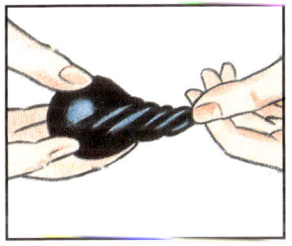

8. Roll a little toilet tissue into a ball and wrap it in the black plastic. Twist the ends tightly and wind with a strip of tape.

9. Push the twisted end into the hole in the snout to make a nose. Then attach it to the inside of the mask with some tape.

49

Bright bird

This vivid bird mask is very comfortable to wear. Make a basic mask out of thin cardboard using the template on page 60. You also need a piece of thin cardboard 18 x 8cm (7 x 3in); about ½ metre (1½ft) medium weight sew-in interfacing*; red and yellow paint and shirring elastic.

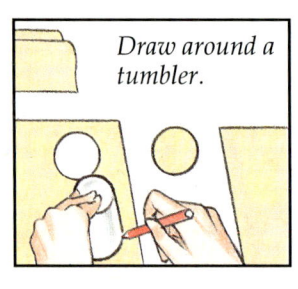

Draw around a tumbler.

1. Cut two pieces of interfacing 45 x 8cm (17¾ x 3in), one piece 20 x 9cm (8 x 3½in) and two circles, 8cm (3in) across.

2. Dip the two pieces of the same size into cold water and squeeze them. Blot the pieces between newspaper.

3. With a fat paintbrush drip yellow and red runny paint onto the damp pieces. The paint will smudge slightly.

The beak

Fold your piece of thin cardboard so the long sides meet. Mark the bottom edge 3cm (1¼in) from the left.

Join the points called A, B and C with a pencil line. Cut along the lines.

Snip 1cm (½in) along the top of the fold and bend the sides to make tabs. Paint it orange and let it dry.

50

* You can buy interfacing in dressmakers' stores.

These are eye pieces.

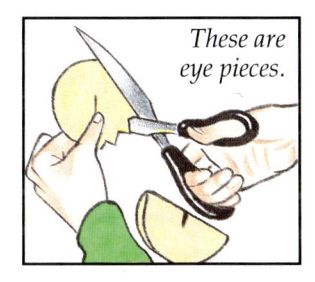

1. Fold the circles in half and snip the middles. Open them out and snip points around the edge of each circle.

5. Paint the circles and the remaining piece of interfacing bright red. Let all the painted pieces dry in a warm place.

Paint black circles on the eye pieces to outline the eyes.

Owl

The owl mask is made in the same way as the bright bird. Use runny brown paint for the speckled feathers and paint the top feathers brown. Paint the eye pieces white. Make a shorter, fatter beak using the template on page 56.

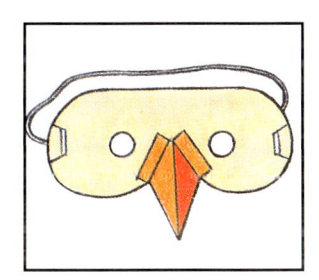

6. Attach the elastic to the basic mask (see page 34). Glue the tabs of the beak 3cm (1¼in) from the top (see box left).

7. Cut the spotted pieces and the red piece into 2½cm (1in) strips. Trim them to make rounded points like feathers.

Cut lots of strips together.

8. Glue four red feathers each side, then five spotted ones either side. Stick three straight up and two down.

9. Glue the rest of the feathers around the eyes and stick on the eye pieces, as shown. Push the scissors into the eye slit to cut out.

51

Goggle-eyed monster

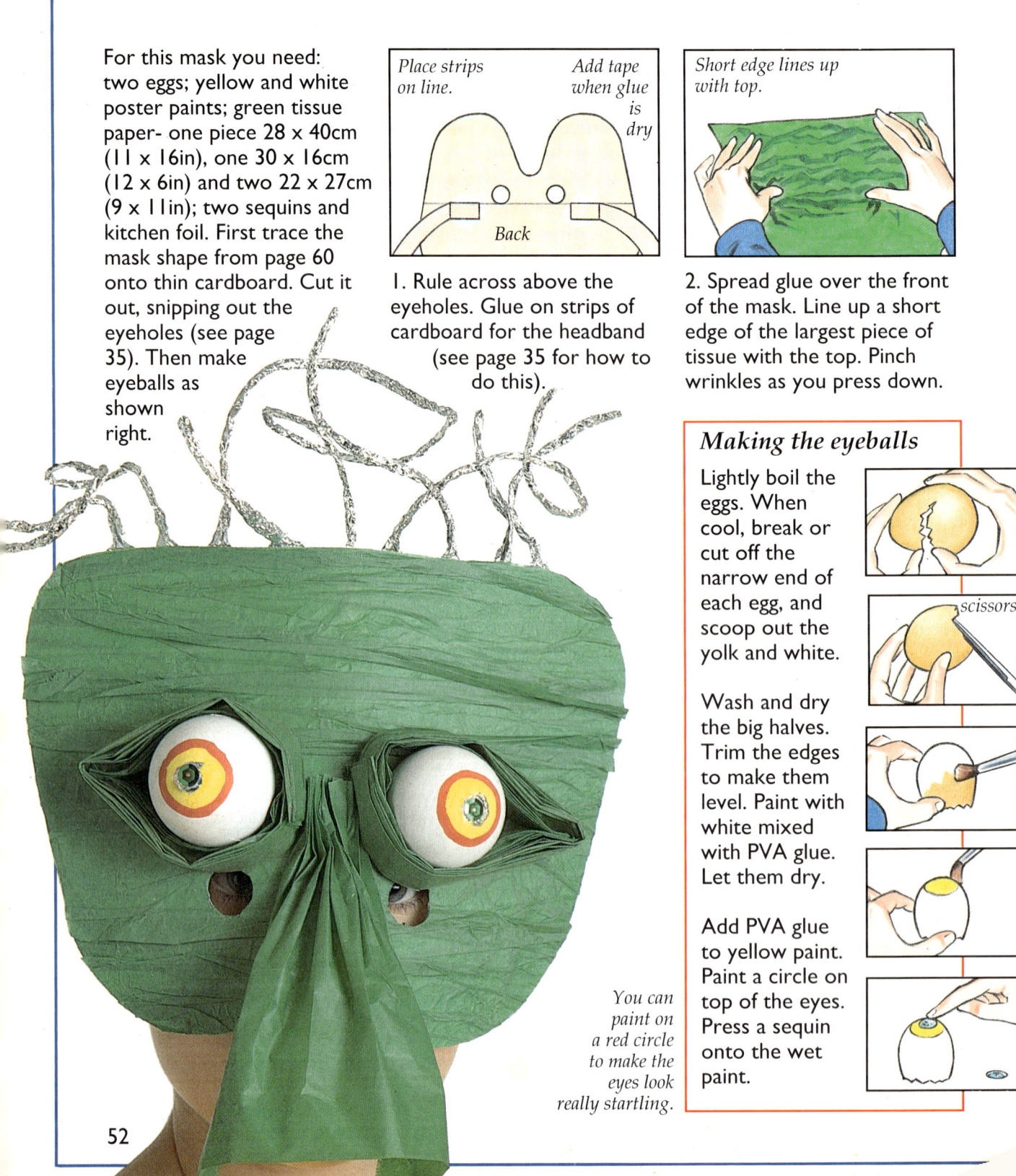

For this mask you need: two eggs; yellow and white poster paints; green tissue paper- one piece 28 x 40cm (11 x 16in), one 30 x 16cm (12 x 6in) and two 22 x 27cm (9 x 11in); two sequins and kitchen foil. First trace the mask shape from page 60 onto thin cardboard. Cut it out, snipping out the eyeholes (see page 35). Then make eyeballs as shown right.

Place strips on line. *Add tape when glue is dry*

Back

1. Rule across above the eyeholes. Glue on strips of cardboard for the headband (see page 35 for how to do this).

Short edge lines up with top.

2. Spread glue over the front of the mask. Line up a short edge of the largest piece of tissue with the top. Pinch wrinkles as you press down.

You can paint on a red circle to make the eyes look really startling.

Making the eyeballs

Lightly boil the eggs. When cool, break or cut off the narrow end of each egg, and scoop out the yolk and white.

scissors

Wash and dry the big halves. Trim the edges to make them level. Paint with white mixed with PVA glue. Let them dry.

Add PVA glue to yellow paint. Paint a circle on top of the eyes. Press a sequin onto the wet paint.

Stick tape half on mask and half on sides of egg.

Pleat on short edges.

These are eyelids.

Try not to crush pleats in the eyelids.

3. When dry, trim the eyeholes and the edges of the mask. Tape the eyeballs above the eyeholes, keeping them level with the strips.

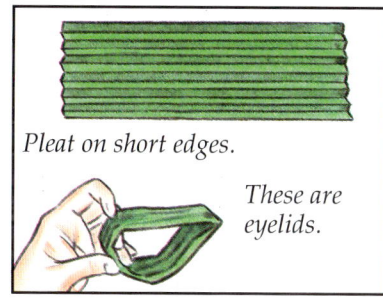

4. Fold the pieces of tissue 22 x 27cm (9 x 11in) into concertina pleats. Fold them in half and pinch the fold. Glue the loose ends together.

5. Glue around the eggs and 2cm (1in) up the sides. Place the eyelids over the eggs, try not to crush the pleats. Press gently onto the mask.

Cyclops

Cyclops was a one-eyed Greek monster.

Use the same steps to make a Cyclops mask, like this, or a three-eyed monster.

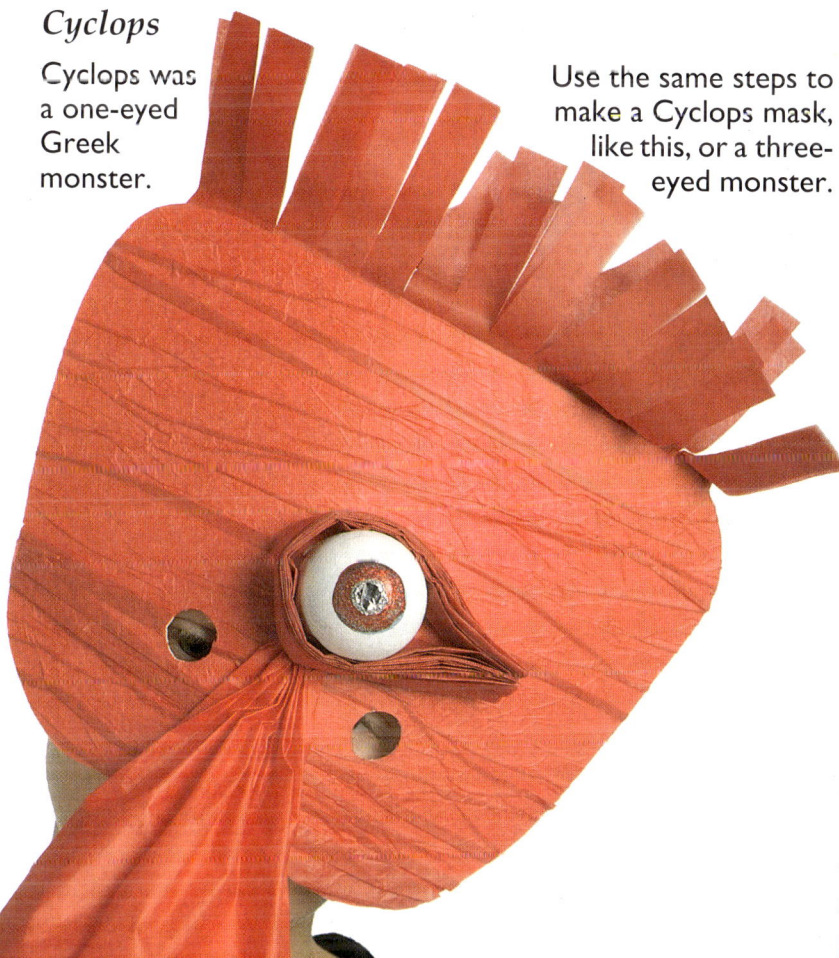

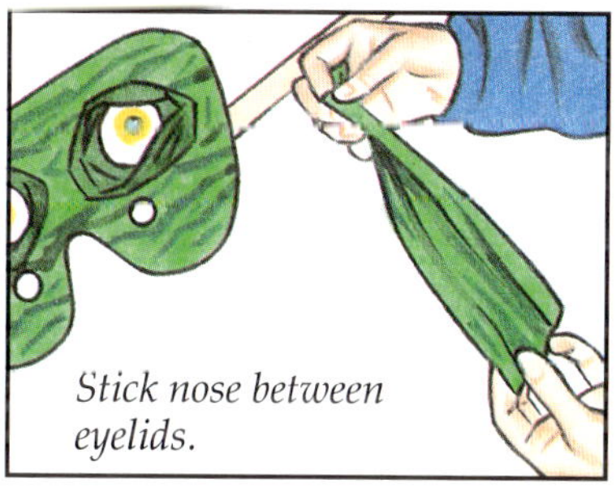

Stick nose between eyelids.

6. Fold the short edges of the last piece of tissue together. Pleat the folded end, squeeze and fold back 2cm (1in). Glue to the mask

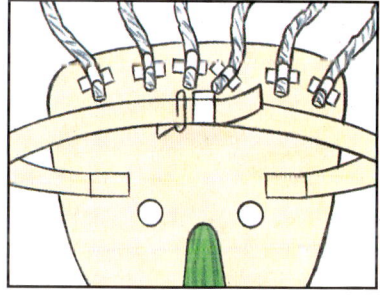

7. Make weird twists of kitchen foil to tape behind the top of the mask. Wrap the strips around your head (see page 35).

53

Dracula

This mask is shaped onto a clay base which you can use again and again. You will need a shallow bowl about 15cm (6in) across; a tray; clingfilm; about 1kg (2lb) self-hardening clay; kitchen foil; a cotton wool ball*; white tissue paper; black yarn; hat elastic and black and red paints.

1. Turn the bowl over and put it on the back of the tray. Cover it all with clingfilm. Roll balls of clay about the size of small oranges.

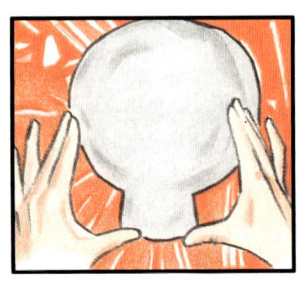

2. Flatten the balls and press them over the bowl. Add a larger ball at one end to shape a chin. Smooth the joins with your thumbs.

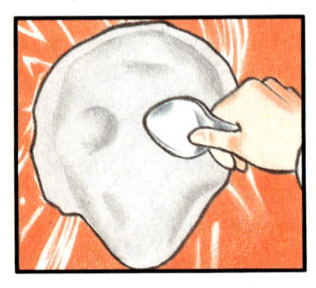

3. About half-way down the face, press in eye sockets with the back of a dessert spoon. Rock the spoon from side to side as you press.

You could paint the eyes like this. Use glitter pen for Dracula's shiny eyeballs.

Add a few drops of red to the fangs.

Eyes
Slightly flatten two marble-sized balls of clay into the sockets.

Eyebrows
Roll sausage shapes. Place them so that they arch.

Lips
Taper the ends of two sausage shapes. The bottom lip should be slightly shorter than the top. Press curves in the top lip. Roll and press on two fangs.

Nose
Make a wedge and pinch it along the top. Smooth two small balls onto each side of the nose for nostrils. Poke your finger in to shape them.

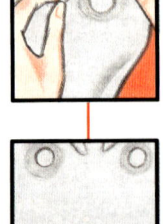

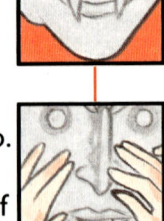

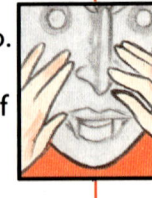

*cotton ball (US)

4. Shape Dracula's features and firmly press them on the face (see box left). Leave in a warm place overnight to dry.

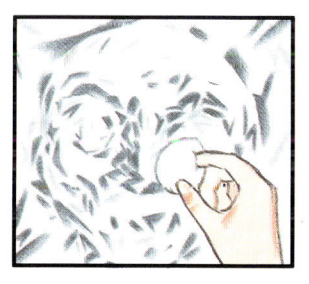

5. Lay foil over the face and press it down, starting with the nose (see Tips). Flatten the creases with cotton wool*.

Sea witch

On the clay base, leave out the fangs and make the mouth smaller. Glue on blue or green tissue paper instead of white. Stick blue glitter on the brows, eyes and mouth. Tape on strips of shiny green paper and gift wrap ribbon for the hair. Glue on shiny cut-out fish.

Tips

If the kitchen foil rips while you are pressing it around the clay base, just dab some glue around the tear and then patch it with a small piece of foil.

As you stick on the tissue paper, add extra squares on the nose, mouth and brows as well as strips along the sides. This makes the mask really strong.

6. Paint PVA glue over the face and around the base. Stick on small squares of tissue paper. Do this four times (see Tips).

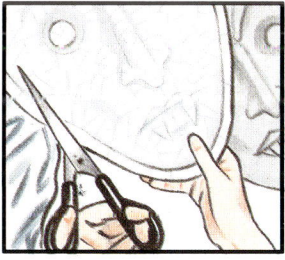

7. When dry, ease the mask off the clay base. Trim the mask, leaving a 1cm (½in) edge. Turn in the edges and press.

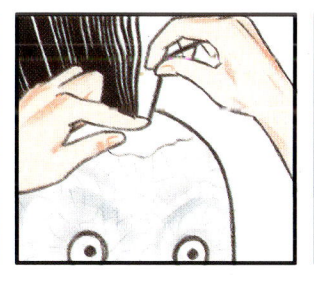

8. Poke in eyeholes with a sharp pencil and add hat elastic (see page 34). Glue on yarn strands in a V-shape for hair.

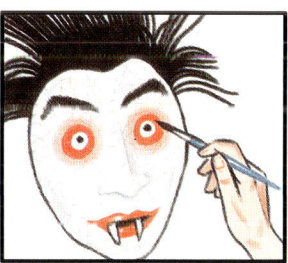

9. With a nearly dry brush, shade around the eyes in red and then paint them as shown. Paint the lips red and the brows black.

55

Templates

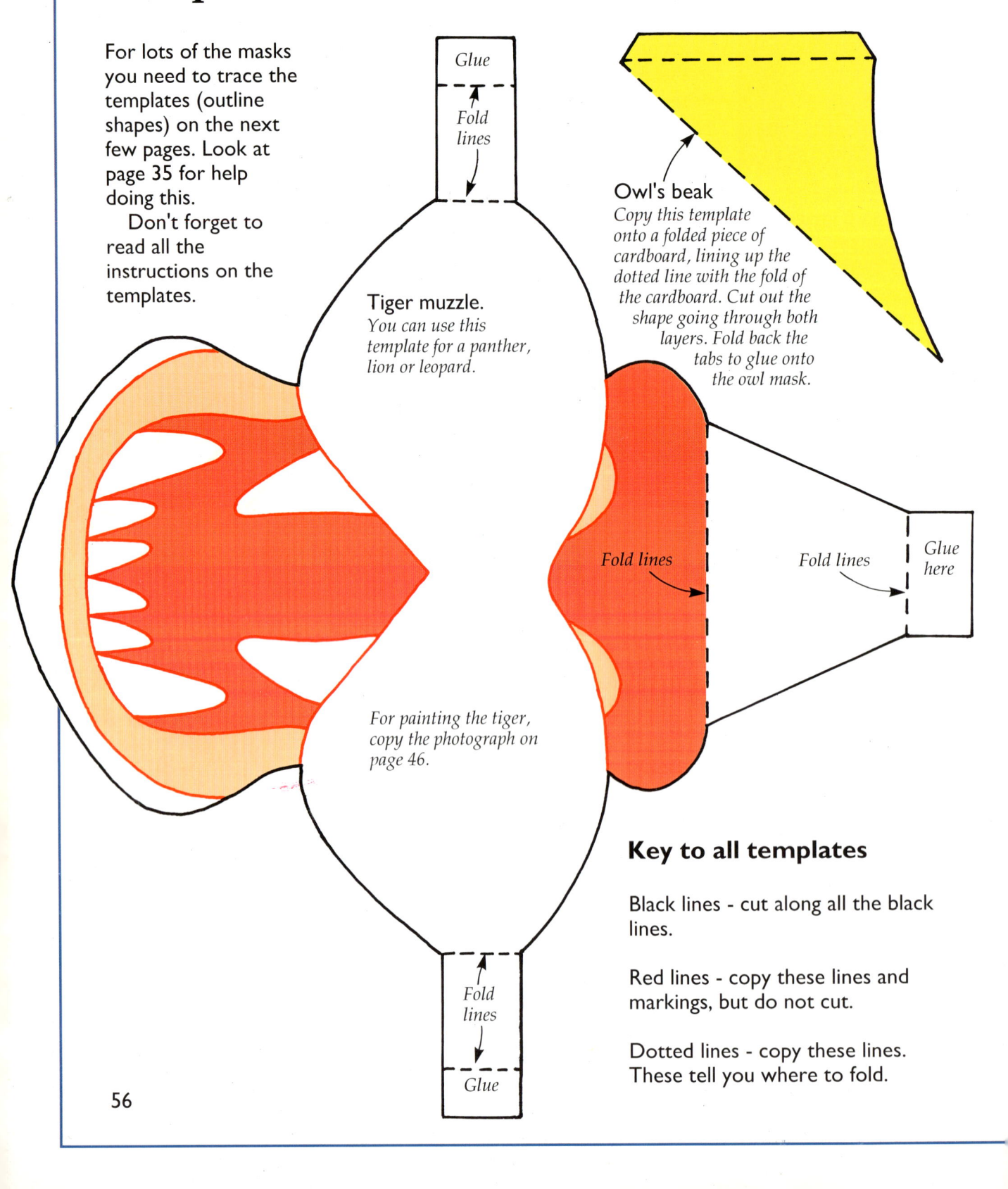

For lots of the masks you need to trace the templates (outline shapes) on the next few pages. Look at page 35 for help doing this.

Don't forget to read all the instructions on the templates.

Glue

Fold lines

Tiger muzzle. *You can use this template for a panther, lion or leopard.*

Owl's beak *Copy this template onto a folded piece of cardboard, lining up the dotted line with the fold of the cardboard. Cut out the shape going through both layers. Fold back the tabs to glue onto the owl mask.*

Fold lines

Fold lines

Glue here

For painting the tiger, copy the photograph on page 46.

Key to all templates

Black lines - cut along all the black lines.

Red lines - copy these lines and markings, but do not cut.

Dotted lines - copy these lines. These tell you where to fold.

Fold lines

Glue

Tiger ears
Copy and cut out two of these.

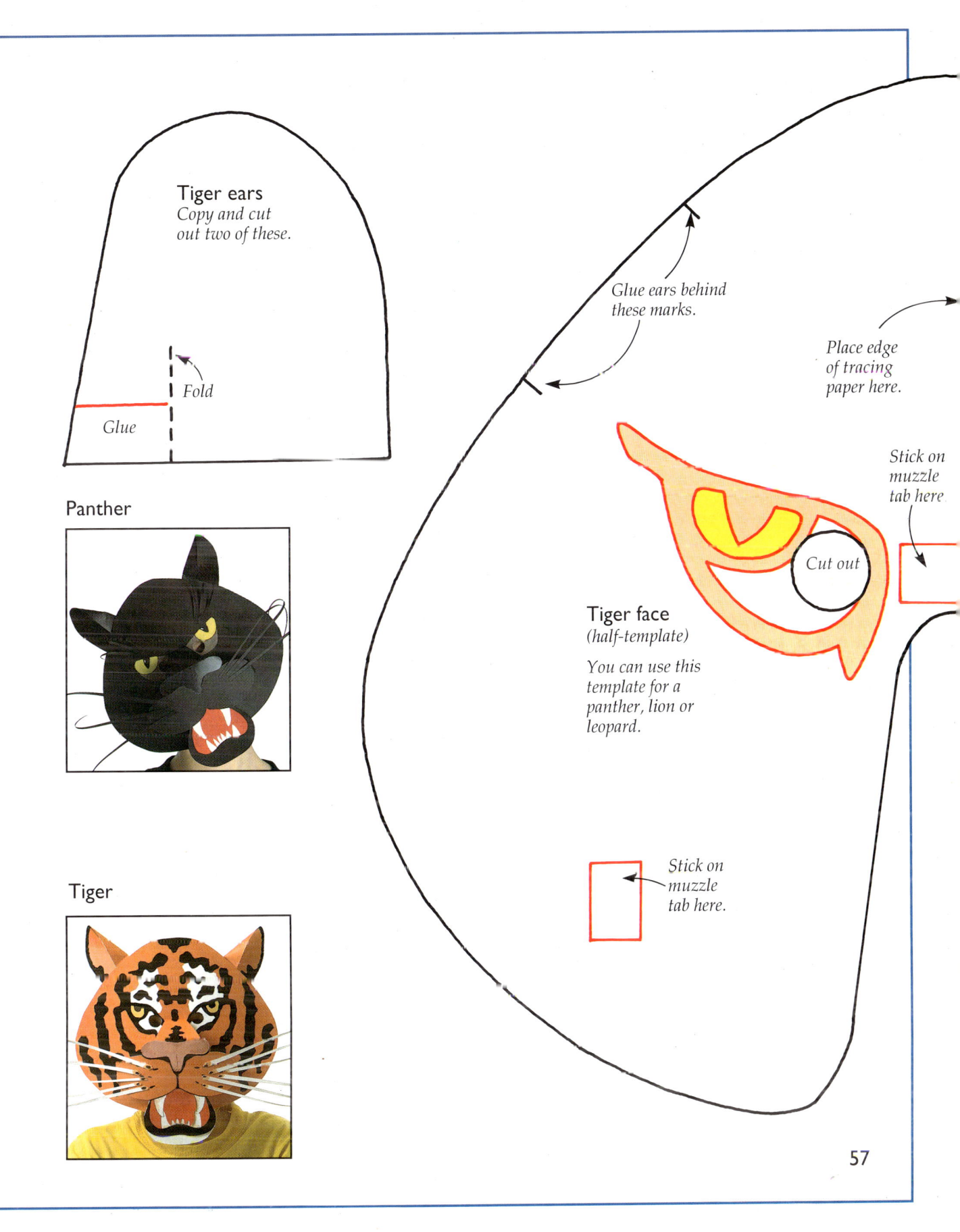

Fold

Glue

Panther

Glue ears behind these marks.

Place edge of tracing paper here.

Stick on muzzle tab here

Cut out

Tiger face
(half-template)

You can use this template for a panther, lion or leopard.

Stick on muzzle tab here.

Tiger

57

Line up fold of tracing paper here.

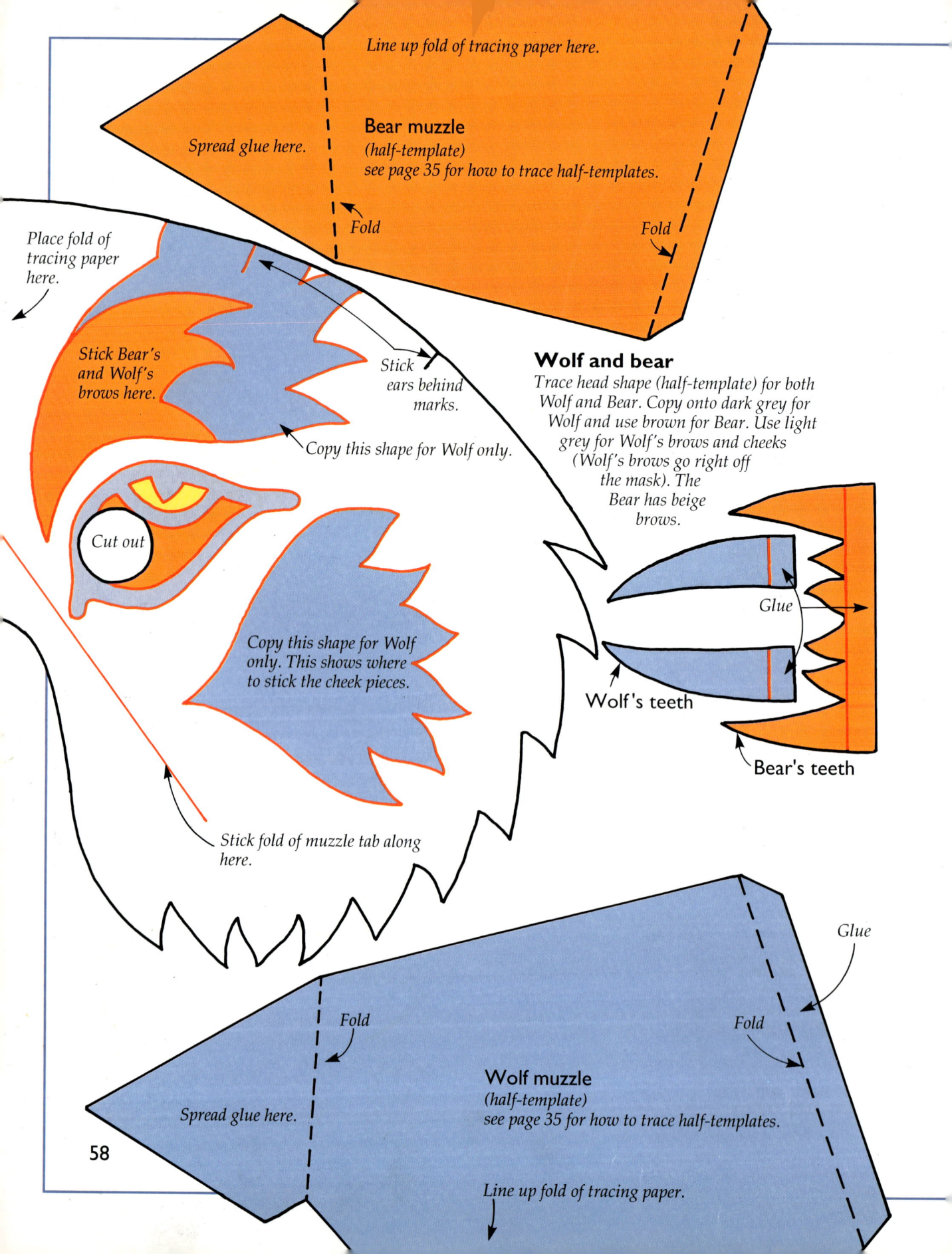

Spread glue here.

Bear muzzle
(half-template)
see page 35 for how to trace half-templates.

Fold

Fold

Place fold of tracing paper here.

Stick Bear's and Wolf's brows here.

Stick ears behind marks.

Copy this shape for Wolf only.

Cut out

Copy this shape for Wolf only. This shows where to stick the cheek pieces.

Wolf and bear
Trace head shape (half-template) for both Wolf and Bear. Copy onto dark grey for Wolf and use brown for Bear. Use light grey for Wolf's brows and cheeks (Wolf's brows go right off the mask). The Bear has beige brows.

Glue

Wolf's teeth

Bear's teeth

Stick fold of muzzle tab along here.

58

Glue

Fold

Fold

Spread glue here.

Wolf muzzle
(half-template)
see page 35 for how to trace half-templates.

Line up fold of tracing paper.

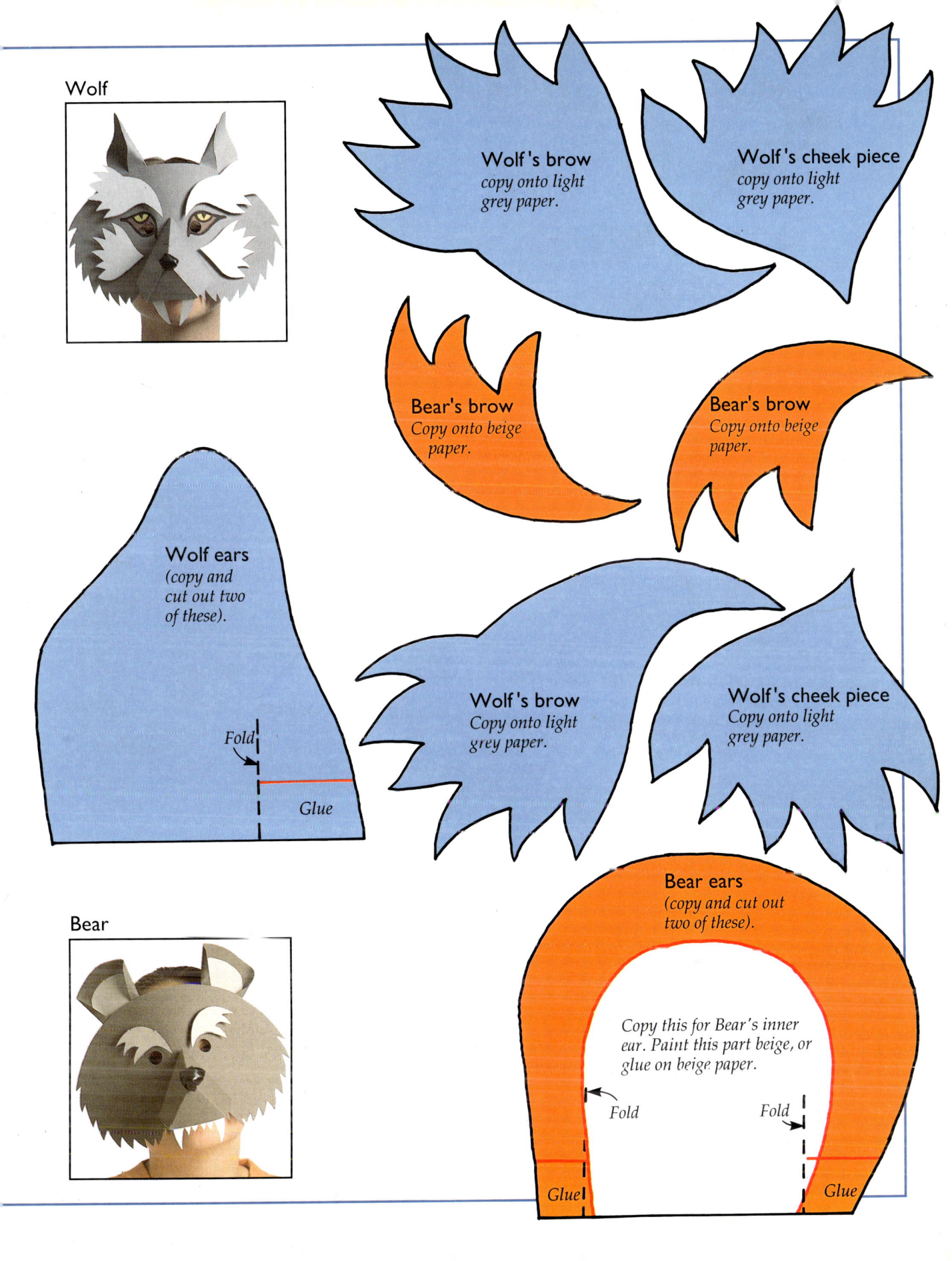

Wolf

Wolf's brow
copy onto light grey paper.

Wolf's cheek piece
copy onto light grey paper.

Bear's brow
Copy onto beige paper.

Bear's brow
Copy onto beige paper.

Wolf ears
(copy and cut out two of these).

Fold

Glue

Wolf's brow
Copy onto light grey paper.

Wolf's cheek piece
Copy onto light grey paper.

Bear

Bear ears
(copy and cut out two of these).

Copy this for Bear's inner ear. Paint this part beige, or glue on beige paper.

Fold

Fold

Glue

Glue

You will need the basic mask shape on this page to make lots of the masks in this book.

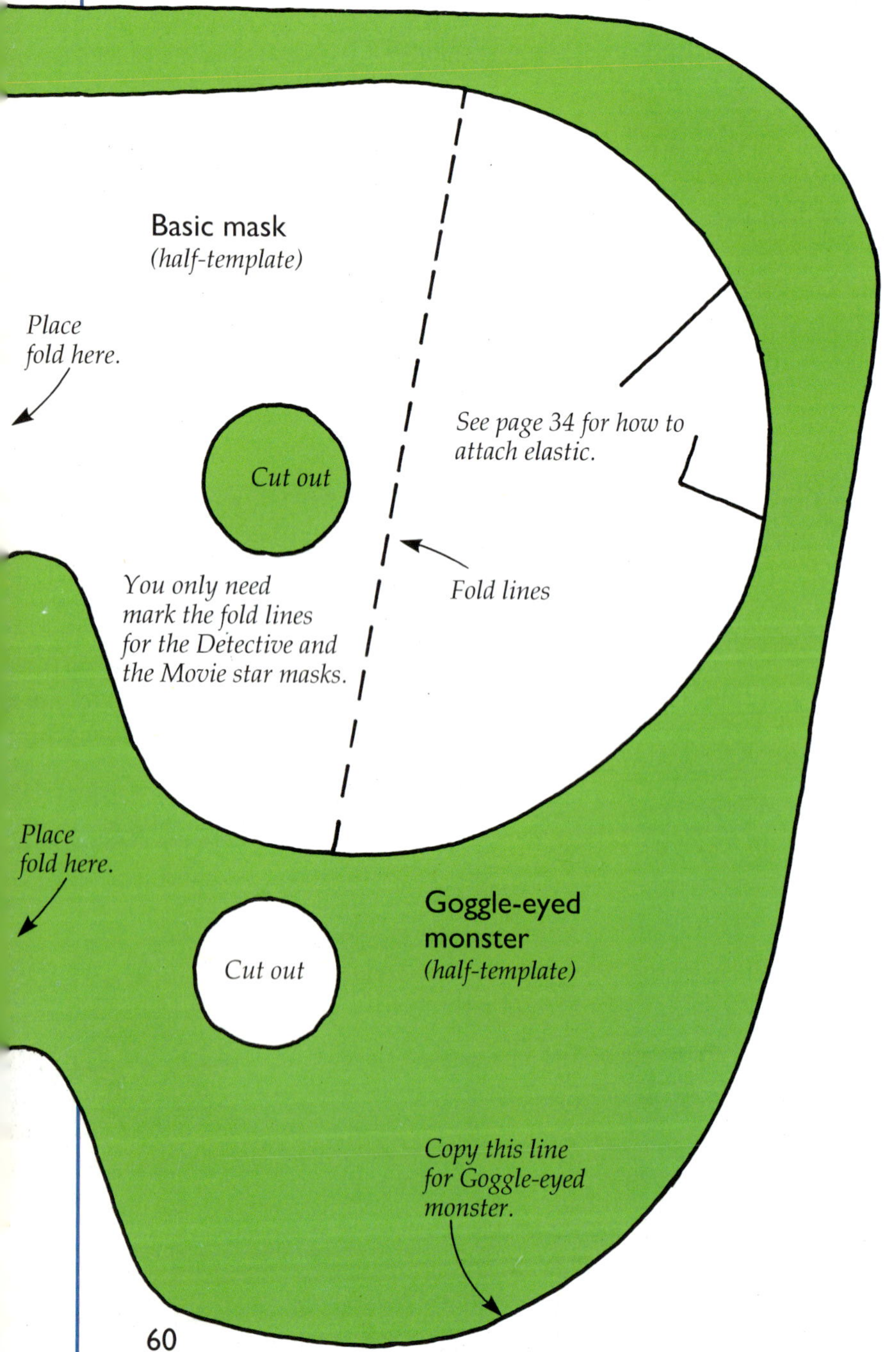

Basic mask
(half-template)

Place fold here.

Cut out

See page 34 for how to attach elastic.

Fold lines

You only need mark the fold lines for the Detective and the Movie star masks.

Place fold here.

Cut out

Goggle-eyed monster
(half-template)

Copy this line for Goggle-eyed monster.

Goggle-eyed monster

Hovering bee
(You need a basic mask for this)

Leaping fish
(you need a basic mask for this)

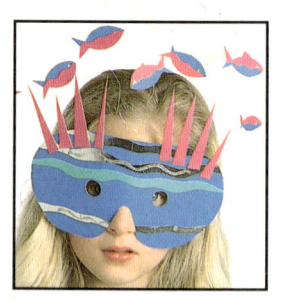

Owl
(you need a basic mask for this)

Bright bird
(you need a basic mask for this)

Place fold here.

Cut out

Movie star
(half-template)
see page 35 for how to trace this.

Detective
(half-template)
see page 35.

Place fold here.

Movie star
(you need a basic mask)

Detective
(you need a basic mask)

Cut out

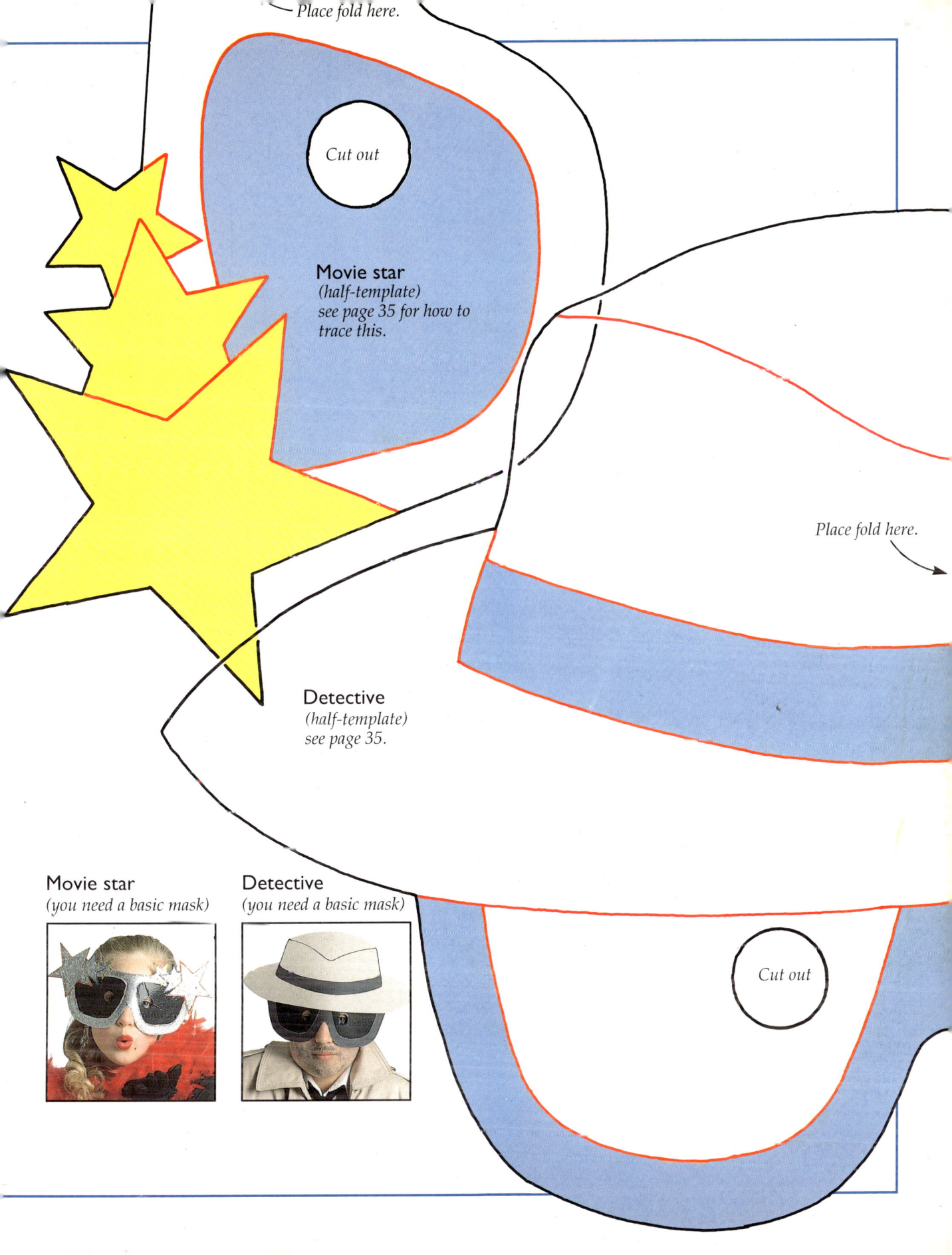

Frankenstein

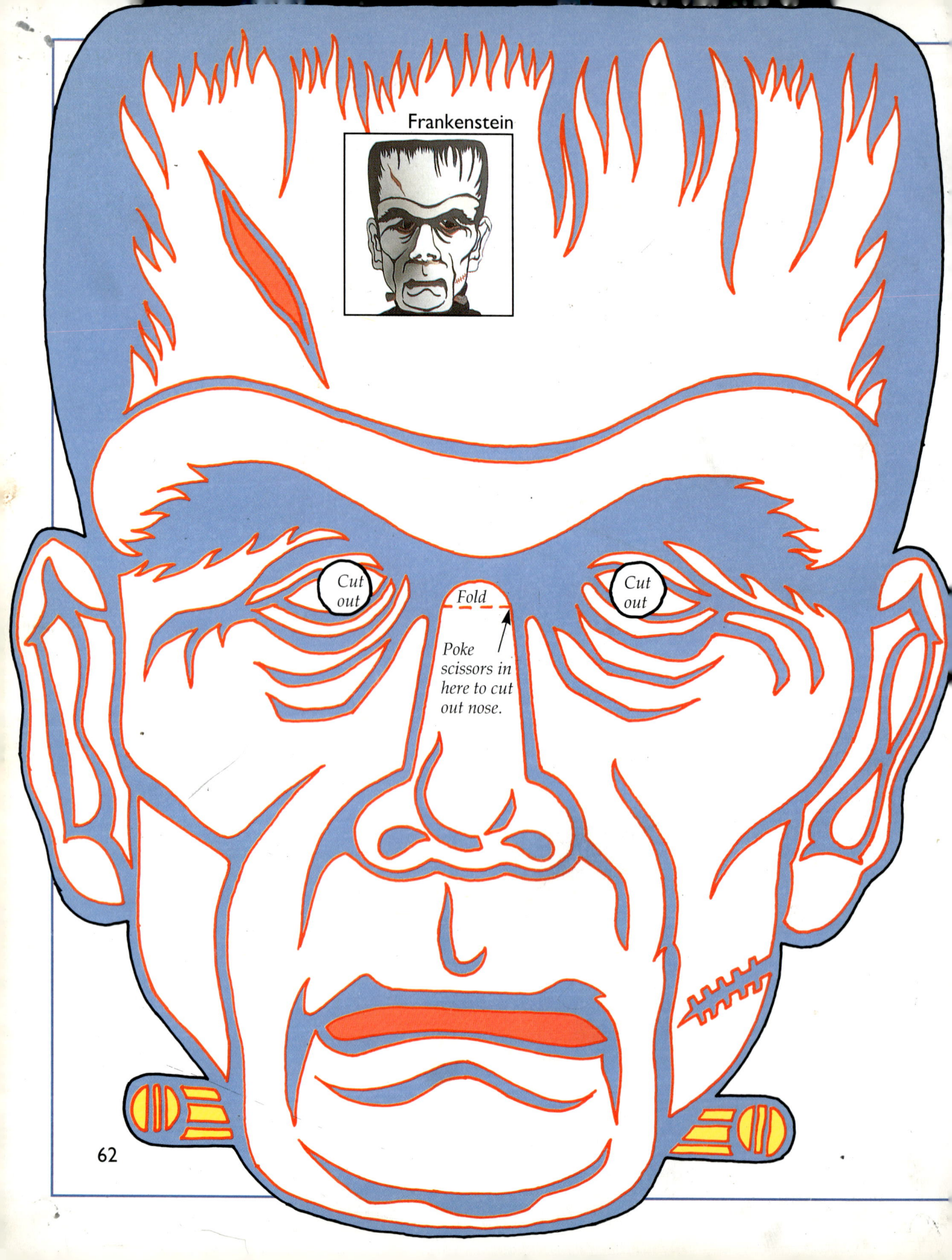

Cut out

Cut out

Fold

Poke scissors in here to cut out nose.

62

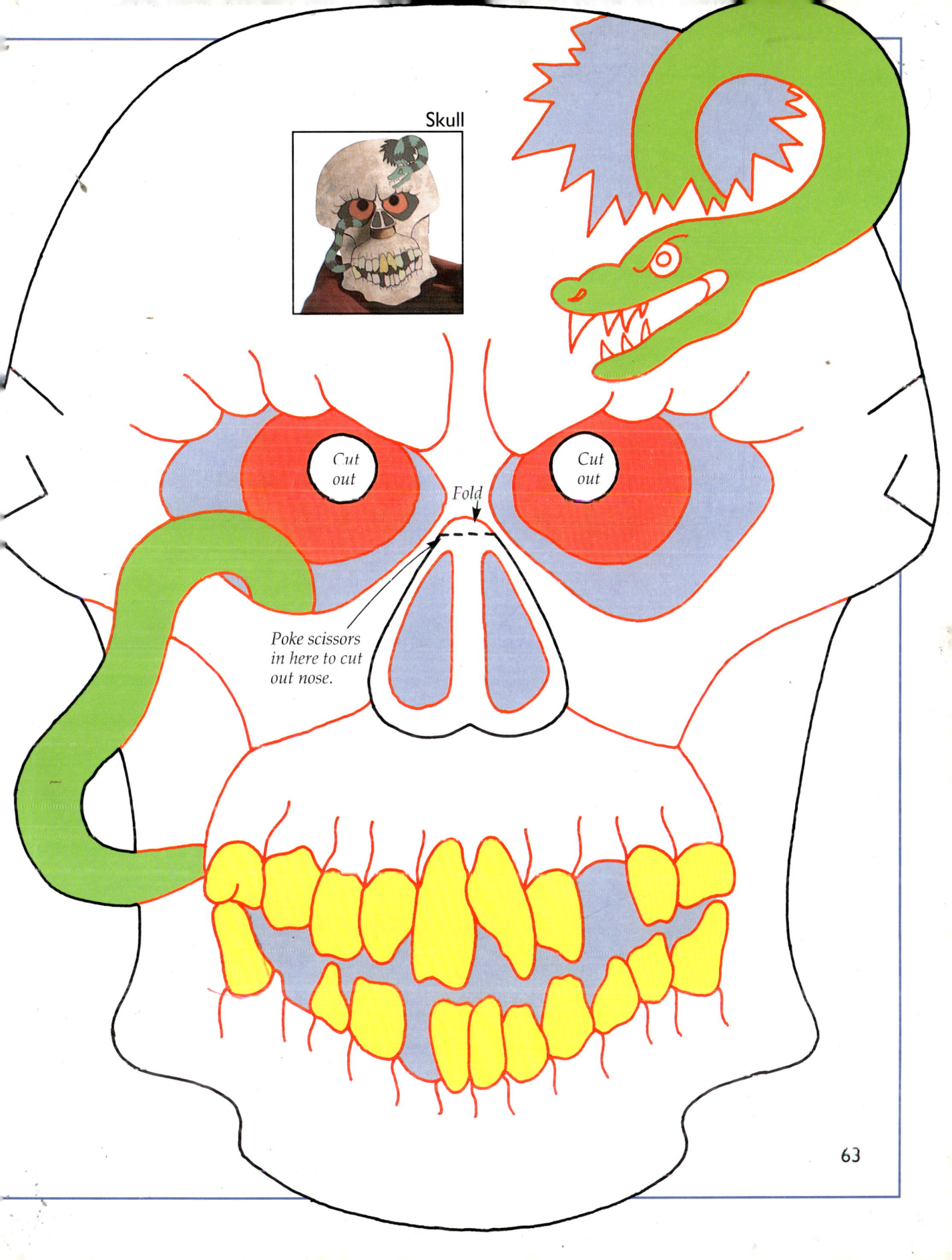

Skull

Cut out

Cut out

Fold

Poke scissors in here to cut out nose.

63

Cut along black lines.

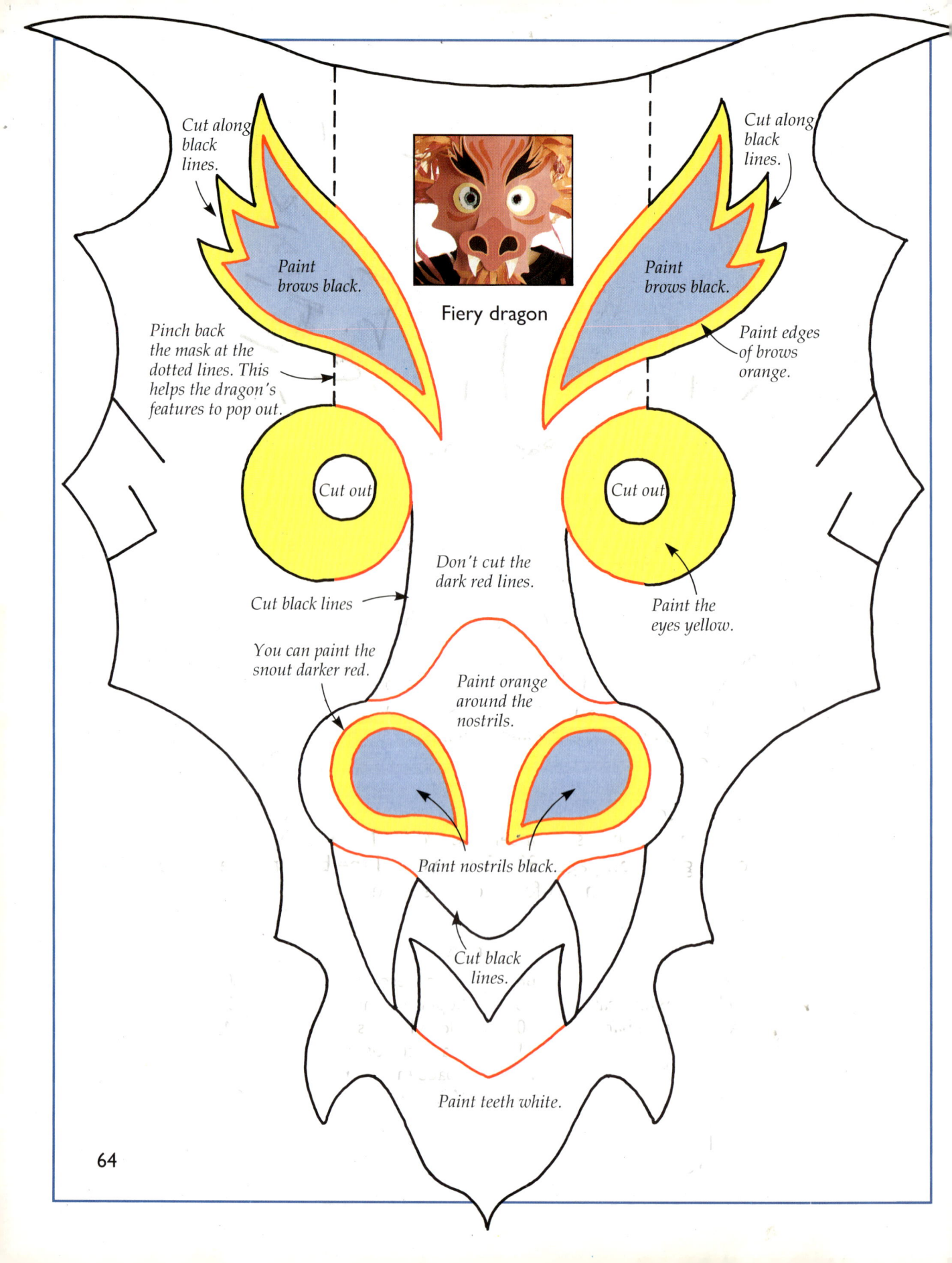

Cut along black lines.

Paint brows black.

Paint brows black.

Fiery dragon

Paint edges of brows orange.

Pinch back the mask at the dotted lines. This helps the dragon's features to pop out.

Cut out

Cut out

Don't cut the dark red lines.

Cut black lines

Paint the eyes yellow.

You can paint the snout darker red.

Paint orange around the nostrils.

Paint nostrils black.

Cut black lines.

Paint teeth white.

64

FANCY DRESS

Ray Gibson

With special thanks to Eliza Borton, Johanna Briscoe, Jonathan Briscoe, Matthew Evans, Ellie Gibson and Harry Gibson.

How to use this book

This part of the book shows you how to make lots of different fancy dress costumes. Most of the costumes are based on clothes that you probably already have, such as T-shirts and sweatshirts. In this part of the book these clothes are called basics. The ones that you need for each costume are shown in a list after the word **Basics.**

You alter the basics or make things to go with them to transform them into the costumes. The parts of each costume that you need to make are listed after the words **To make.**

The shopping lists on pages 92-93 tell you all the bits and pieces you need for each costume.

Contents

Clown	66	Superhero	80
Black-and-white cat	68	Superheroine	82
Giant vampire bat	70	More heroes	84
Butterfly	71	Mad scientist	85
Skeleton	72	Space monster	86
Boxer	74	Wizard	88
Back-to-front person	75	Comic waiter	90
Headless man	76	Shopping lists	92
Scarecrow	79	Templates	94

Clown

Basics: bright T-shirt; man's big, old trousers; bright tights; clashing socks; gym shoes or trainers; white gloves; any hat.
To make: bow tie; collar; hair; flower; buttons; braces. Find out exactly what materials you need for these on page 92.

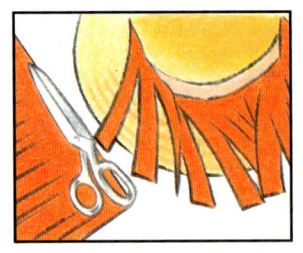

1. Snip along one long edge of tissue strips 20cm (8in) wide. Tape in layers into the hat, with a gap for the face.

You could paint a clown's face with face paint (see pages 10-11), or wear a clown mask instead (page 41).

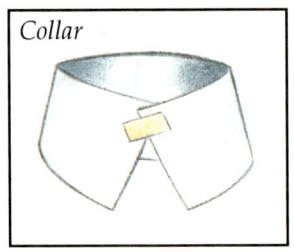

Collar

2. Cut a strip of white cardboard to fit your neck loosely. When you put it on, tape the top corners together.

3. Fold a big crepe paper bow. Add self-adhesive spots and stars. Fasten bow to collar with sticky tabs.

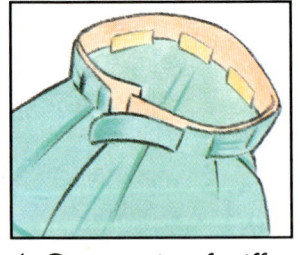

4. Cut a strip of stiff cardboard to fit inside the trousers' waistband. Tape or staple it into position.

5. Cut out and sew or stick bright felt shapes onto the trousers; or use any other bright scraps.

Two holes to sew them on with.

6. Cut two paper cups off about 1cm (½in) from the base. Poke holes in them with a sharp pencil.

Spread out the snips for petals.

7. For the flower, snip along a long piece of tissue paper 8cm (3in) wide. Roll it up and tape the end.

Tape green tissue paper leaves to your flower, if you like.

You could hold an eye-catching helium balloon.

Cut legs of old trousers off in jagged shapes.

Keep an eye open in charity shops for big, bright, old clothes. You should be able to find things that are not expensive.

The brighter the clothes you wear and the more they clash, the better your clown will look.

Putting the costume together

You will need someone to help you put this costume on. Put on the T-shirt, tights, socks and shoes first. Then follow these steps to put the rest together.

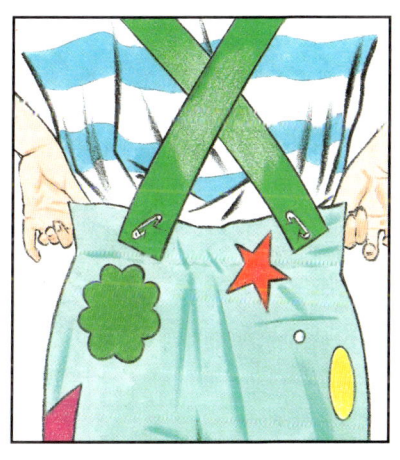

Pull the trousers on. Hold them up at your waist level. Ask someone to safety pin the ribbons to the waist at the back. Slant them inward.

Cross the ribbons at the back and pull them over your shoulders. Pin them, the same distance apart as at the back, to the waist at the front.

Paint the buttons brightly. Sew them on over the ends of the ribbons, through the holes. Use a darning needle and clashing yarn.

Put on the collar and bow tie so they hang loosely around your neck. Stick or staple the flower to the hat. Put the hat and gloves on last.

67

Black-and-white cat

Basics: black sweatshirt and thick, black tights, or black tracksuit bottoms; thick, white socks; white gloves.
To make: mask; bib; collar; tail; fish. Find out what materials you need on page 92.

Before you start

Cut wadding 19 x 23cm (7½ x 9in); fur fabric 70 x 20cm (28 x 8in) and another piece 40 x 10cm (16 x 4in). Put them aside and keep the scraps. Trace and cut out the cat mask template on page 96 in thin, black cardboard.

Mask

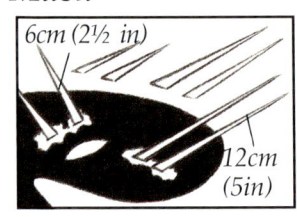

1. Cut whiskers in white cardboard. Do four long, thin ones and four short ones. Glue on, as shown.

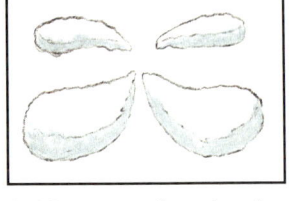

2. Cut out the cheeks and brows in spare wadding. Turn over one of each shape to make mirror images.

3. Pinch and pull the wadding to fluff it up. Glue shapes over the whiskers to meet between the eyes.

4. Trace and cut out the ear patterns as described on page 96. Pin both to fur fabric and cut them out.

5. Tease out scraps of wadding and glue them down the middle of each ear, on the non-furry side.

6. Fold the ears opposite ways at the dotted line and staple. Staple the ears behind the mask, as marked.

Tail

Take the fur fabric 70 x 20cm (28 x 8in). On the non-furry side, put a lot of glue along a long edge. Roll it up longways from the unglued edge. Glue teased-out points of wadding to one end.

Bib

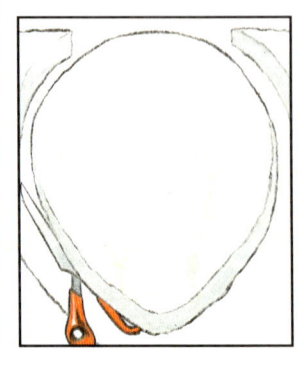

1. Draw lightly with a felt-tip pen, then cut out, a teardrop shape on the wadding 19 x 23cm (7½ x 9in). Fluff it out.

2. Glue more teased-out strips on top, down the middle of the bib. Safety-pin the bib to the sweatshirt from the inside.

Collar

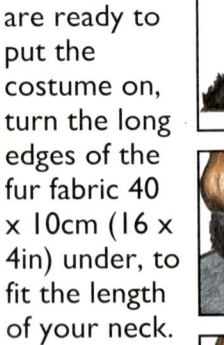

When you are ready to put the costume on, turn the long edges of the fur fabric 40 x 10cm (16 x 4in) under, to fit the length of your neck. Wrap it around your neck and safety-pin at the back.

Fish

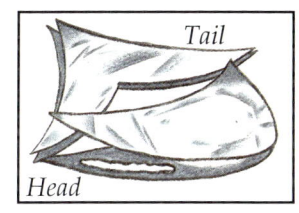

Draw, then cut, two fish heads and two tails in foil. Glue each pair together, with wadding in the head.

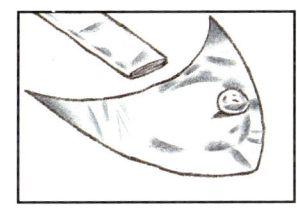

Glue foil balls on for eyes. Fold a foil strip 25cm (10in) long a few times as a spine. Staple on the head and tail.

Fold several strips of foil, each a bit shorter than the last. Fold them into a V-shape like this, for ribs.

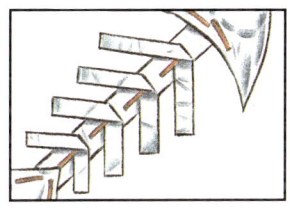

Staple them to the spine about 3cm (1in) apart. Put the biggest near the head, then in size order.

You could paint a black nose, or do a whole cat face with face paints, as on page 7.

Glue sequins around the eyes to outline them, if you want to.

Add extra whiskers, if you like.

Put basic costume (except gloves) on first. Put on the mask and gloves last

Thread elastic through elastic holes on mask, to fit around head.

Pin the tail on from the inside with two safety pins.

Tape a long thread to the fish head and tie the other end to your finger.

Attach tail to your wrist with elastic, if you like.

Wear thick, white socks rolled down to ankles.

Giant vampire bat

Basics: black sweatshirt, tracksuit bottoms, gloves, socks and gym shoes.
To make: wings; cap. See what you need to make these in the list on page 92.

To make the cap

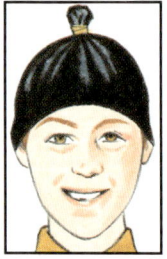

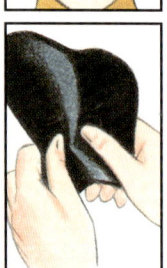

Cut the legs off the tights. Put the top part on your head. Tie the ends with a rubber band and cut off any extra. Turn inside out. Trace the ear template (page 96) and cut two black felt ears. Stretch gently with your thumbs to hollow them out. Fold one side of each ear in as marked. Sew onto tights' waistband 10cm (4in) apart.

Pull cap over ears to hide hair.

Buy plastic vampire fangs and a black eye mask from a joke shop, if you like; or paint them on with face paints. See page 29 for one way to do it.

Wear black socks rolled down, and black gym shoes.

Get help to tape or safety pin the straight edge of the wings along your arms and back from wrist to wrist.

Wings

Follow steps 2 to 5 on the right to make the wing shapes for both costumes. Step 1 shows how to prepare a big, black plastic bag for the bat's wings. You use net for the butterfly's. See the page opposite for how to decorate the butterfly's wings.

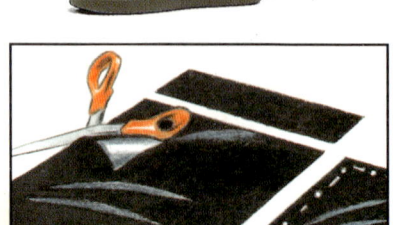

1. Lay the plastic bag flat. Cut off the sealed end. Slit up one side and flatten out the folds. Re-fold in half and pin.

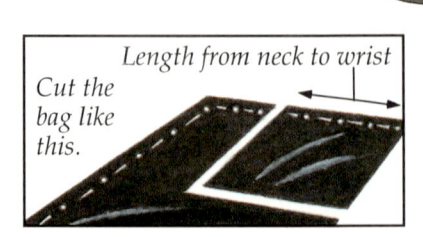

Length from neck to wrist
Cut the bag like this.

2. Ask a friend to measure you from the base of your neck to one wrist. Cut the bag or net into a square this size.

Butterfly

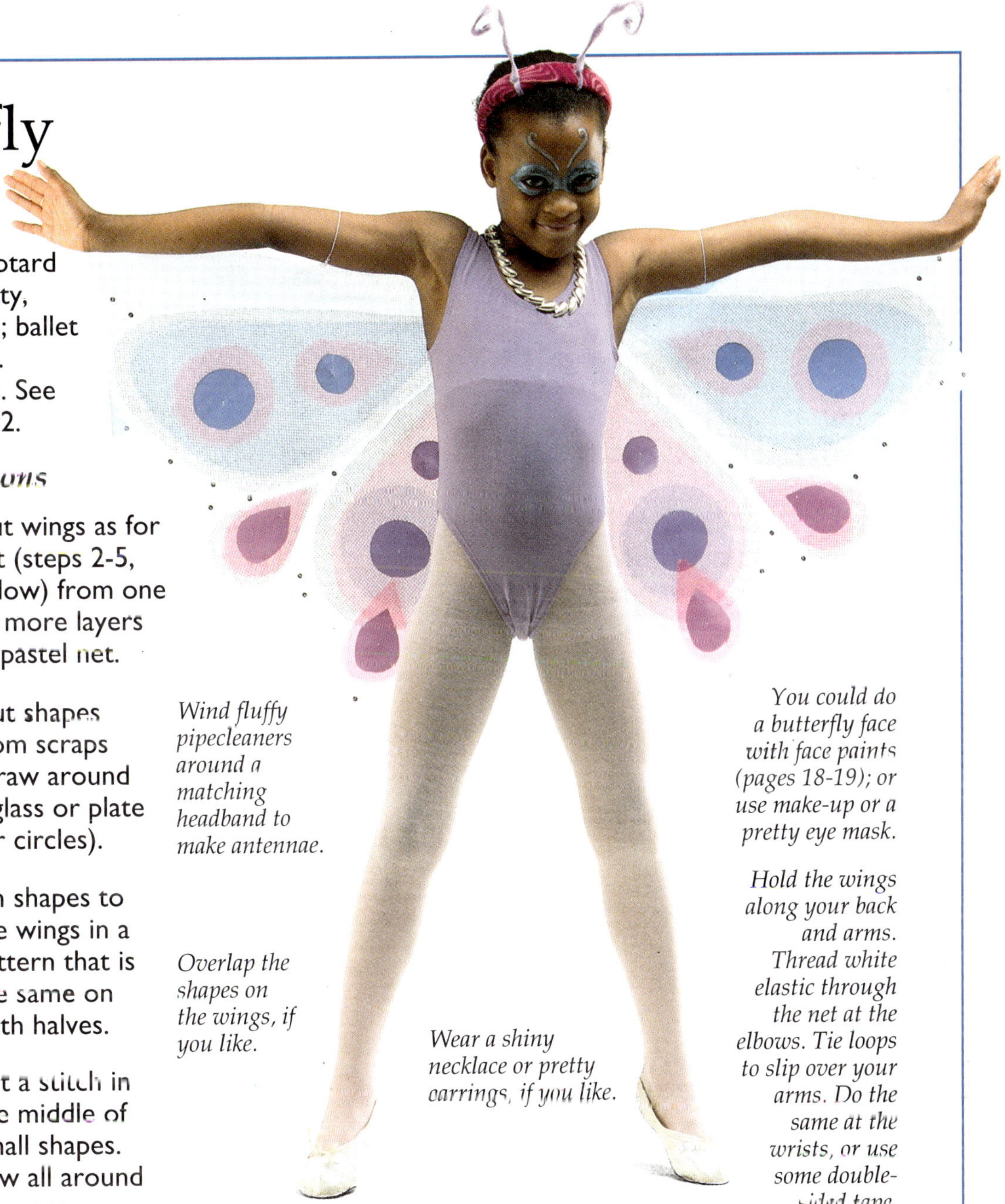

Basics: pastel leotard or swimsuit; pretty, contrasting tights; ballet shoes or slippers.
To make: wings. See the list on page 92.

Wing decorations

Cut wings as for bat (steps 2-5, below) from one or more layers of pastel net.

Cut shapes from scraps (draw around a glass or plate for circles).

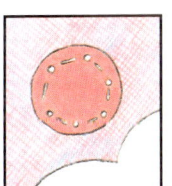

Pin shapes to the wings in a pattern that is the same on both halves.

Put a stitch in the middle of small shapes. Sew all around big ones.

Wind fluffy pipecleaners around a matching headband to make antennae.

Overlap the shapes on the wings, if you like.

Wear a shiny necklace or pretty earrings, if you like.

You could do a butterfly face with face paints (pages 18-19); or use make-up or a pretty eye mask.

Hold the wings along your back and arms. Thread white elastic through the net at the elbows. Tie loops to slip over your arms. Do the same at the wrists, or use some double-sided tape.

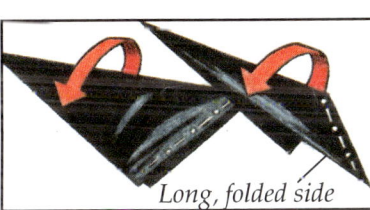

Long, folded side

Small triangle

3. Fold the top right corner to the bottom left one and pin. Take the long, folded side to meet the left edge.

4. Turn the plastic or net over. Pin the smaller top layer to the rest. Cut off the small triangle at the bottom.

5. Draw a curve between the corners of the short edge with a ballpoint pen. Cut off the curve and open out.

71

Skeleton

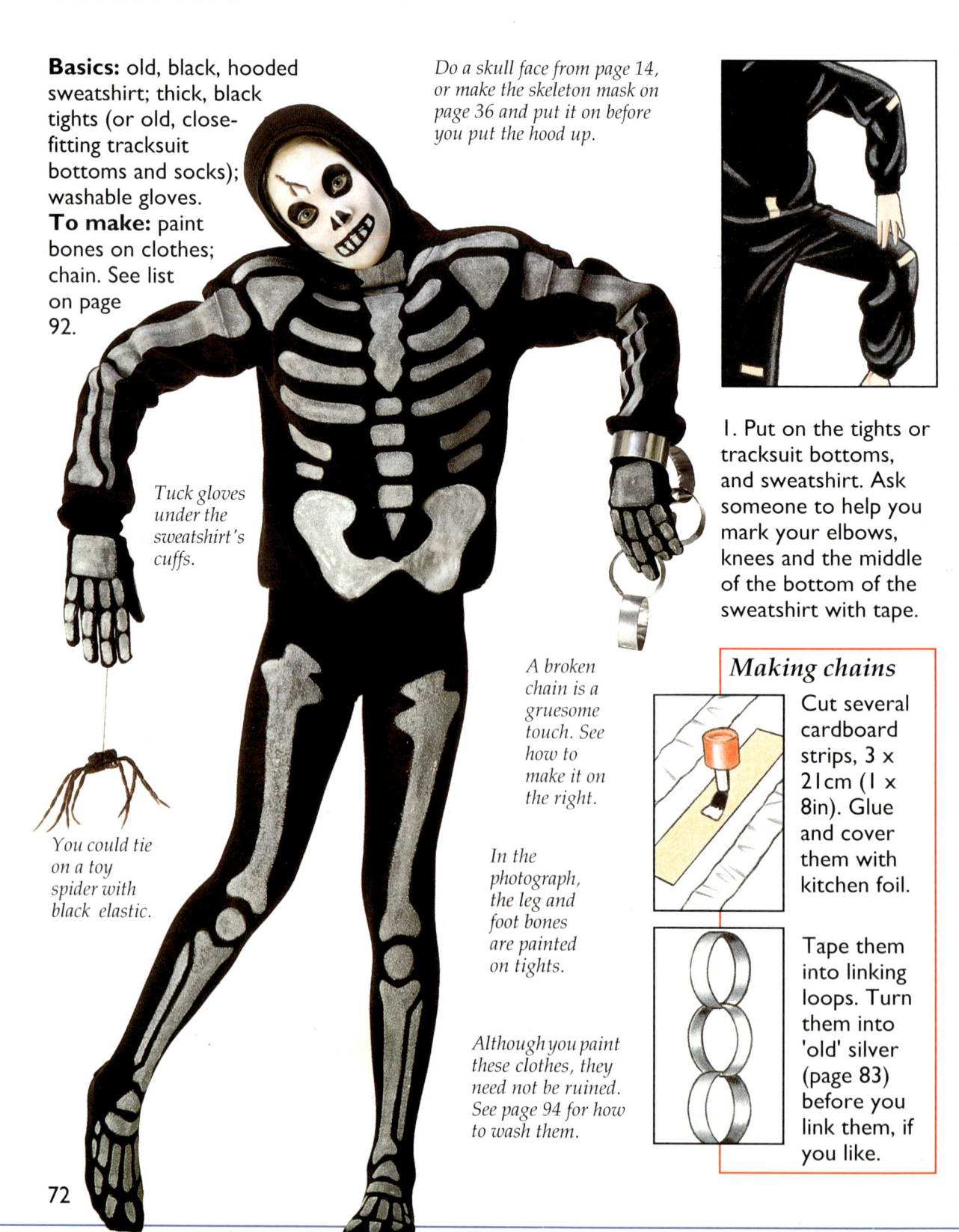

Basics: old, black, hooded sweatshirt; thick, black tights (or old, close-fitting tracksuit bottoms and socks); washable gloves.
To make: paint bones on clothes; chain. See list on page 92.

Do a skull face from page 14, or make the skeleton mask on page 36 and put it on before you put the hood up.

Tuck gloves under the sweatshirt's cuffs.

You could tie on a toy spider with black elastic.

A broken chain is a gruesome touch. See how to make it on the right.

In the photograph, the leg and foot bones are painted on tights.

Although you paint these clothes, they need not be ruined. See page 94 for how to wash them.

1. Put on the tights or tracksuit bottoms, and sweatshirt. Ask someone to help you mark your elbows, knees and the middle of the bottom of the sweatshirt with tape.

Making chains

Cut several cardboard strips, 3 x 21cm (1 x 8in). Glue and cover them with kitchen foil.

Tape them into linking loops. Turn them into 'old' silver (page 83) before you link them, if you like.

72

2. Safety-pin the side edges of the hood under your chin so it fits snugly around your face. Take the shirt off and stitch the edges together with black thread.

3. Lay the sweatshirt flat. Roll up old newspapers to stuff in the sleeves. Press them as flat as you can. Fold newspaper to stuff inside the body too.

How to paint the bones

Mix white paint with a little water to make it creamy. Copy the shapes shown in this picture. Don't worry if they don't come out exactly like this. They will still look like a skeleton.

Collar bone

There is one upper arm bone.

There are two smaller bones in the lower arm.

Ribs

Spine

Do a patch on top of the hand.

Lines of small blobs make finger bones.

Pelvis. Put this on sweatshirt.

Thigh bone has lumpy ends.

Knees

There are two thinner bones below the knee.

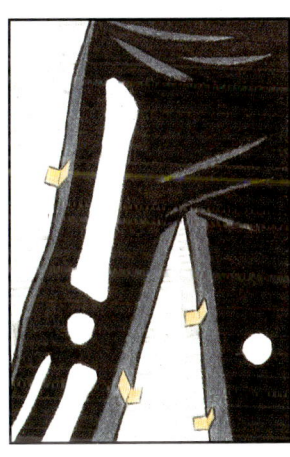

4. Lay the shirt on some newspaper. Tape it down to hold it in place. Paint the bones, as shown on the right, with a small decorator's brush.

5. Stuff the tights or tracksuit bottoms with rolled-up newspaper. Paint the leg bones as shown on the right. Start with the knees.

Remove plastic bag when paint is dry.

6. Paint hand bones on the gloves. Put a plastic bag on your foot, then the sock or tights foot. Paint the foot bones. Use the smaller paintbrush.

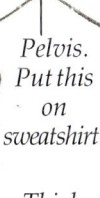

Make feet bones smaller and smaller nearer the toes.

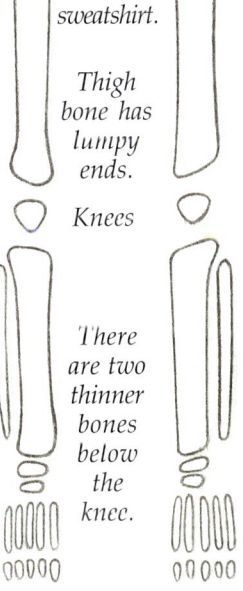

73

Boxer

Basics: plain, bright dressing gown (a silky one is good); shorts that match; black or white gym shoes or trainers, with white laces; sports socks; two bandages.
To make: belt; initials for robe. Look at the list on page 92 to see exactly what you need.

Add a trickle of blood if you have red face paint.

Put gel on hair and slick back from face.

Dab on grey, mauve and green face paint or eye shadow for a bruise.

Wrap belt around waist and tape in position.

Robe

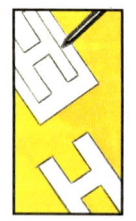

With a felt-tip pen, draw your initials on the felt squares. Cut out.

Cut a small felt square from the scraps, to go after each letter,

Stick to back of robe with double-sided tape.

Tape one end of a bandage to each palm. Ask a friend to wrap them tightly around your hands and wrists. Fasten with safety pins.

Twist strips of kitchen foil and glue them around the medal for decoration. Add extra twists and loops, if you like.

Champion's belt

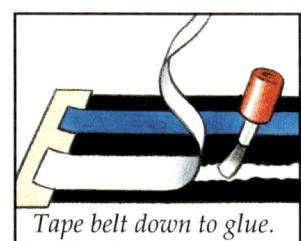

Tape belt down to glue.

1. Paint glue along the black cardboard. Press on the blue and white ribbons, as shown. Wipe off any extra glue with a dry cloth.

Stick shoulder pads in the robe, if you like.

2. When it is dry, staple the fringing or braid below the white ribbon. Cover the staples at the back with tape.

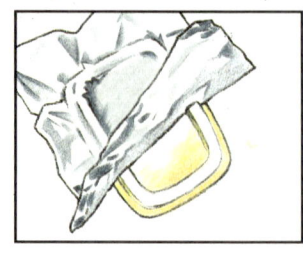

3. Paint glue thickly on the margarine lid. Press kitchen foil over it, tuck the edges under and fasten with tape.

Back-to-front person

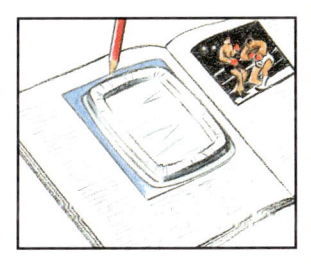

4. Place the lid on top of your picture of a boxer. Draw around it with a pencil and cut out the shape.

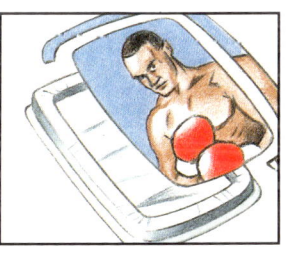

5. Trim another ½cm (¼in) off all around your picture. Glue it to the middle of the lid, so the foil makes a frame around it.

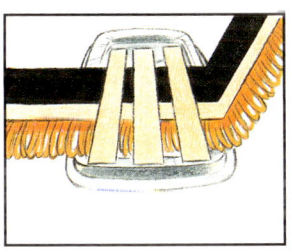

6. Lay the middle of the belt over the lid (both face-down) and tape. Bend the ends of the belt up so medal lies flat when it is on.

This costume works best if you wear formal clothes because casual clothes look much the same from front and back. The same joke works really well for other costumes, too. Try a back-to-front monster with a mask (see pages 36, 52-53, 86), for example.

Basics: shirt; tie; jacket; skirt; socks or tights and shoes.
To make: changes to mask. See page 92 for what you need.

Improving a mask

Lightly scratch the surface of a plastic mask with fine sandpaper.

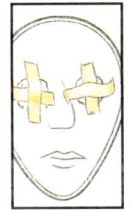

Tape paper over the eye holes from behind. Paint eyeballs on the fronts.

Paint the cheeks, brows and mouth. Use paint and glue mixed.

For the best effect, hold your head back so the mask's chin stays down.

Glasses on the mask can add to the effect.

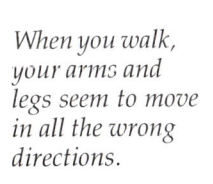

When you walk, your arms and legs seem to move in all the wrong directions.

Here you can see what the model looks like when she turns around.

Getting ready

Put a shirt, tie, jacket and skirt on back to front. You will need some help to button the shirt and knot the tie.

Put a face mask on the back of your head. Arrange hair around it so it looks natural. You could wear a wig if you like.

75

Headless man

See page 92 for everything you need, then follow all the steps on the next three pages.

Basics: black tracksuit bottoms; white T-shirt; black boots; brooch.
To make: head; shoulder frame; changes to big, old, man's, white shirt; boot tops; sash.

To prepare the shirt

Bend the cardboard 60 x 5cm (24 x 2in) around to fit almost double inside the collar. Staple ends.

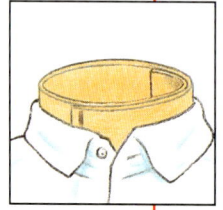

Make the shirt collar stand up and staple the points together. Snip the edge into jagged shapes.

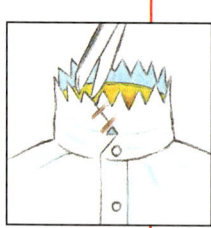

Staple the ring inside the collar and cut off any cardboard that still shows above the jagged edge.

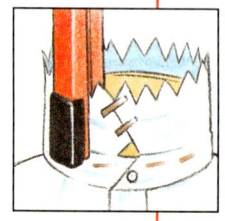

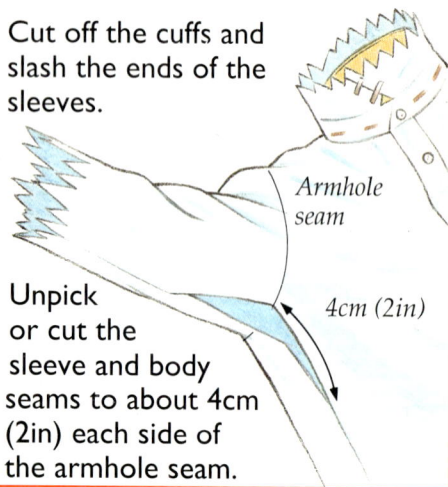

Cut off the cuffs and slash the ends of the sleeves.

Armhole seam

4cm (2in)

Unpick or cut the sleeve and body seams to about 4cm (2in) each side of the armhole seam.

Shoulder frame

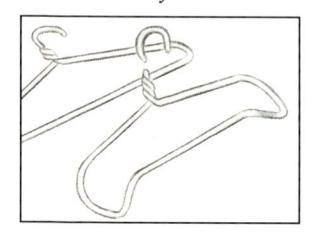

1. Pull a wire hanger into a rectangle. Bend the ends down. Twist to break off the hook. You may need adult help to do this. Bend the spike upright.

2. Wrap the spike in lots of tape. If your sponge is more than 2.5cm (1in) deep, ask an adult to slice it across with a knife to this thickness.

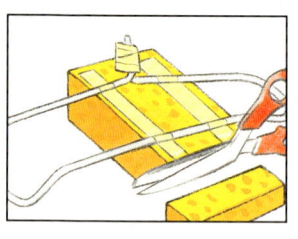

3. Lay the sponge under the hanger. If it sticks out more than 1.5cm (¾in), trim it with scissors. Tape it on well, right around the wire.

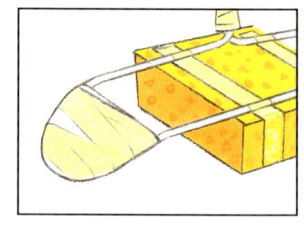

4. Tape a shoulder pad over each end of the hanger. Hang the shirt over the frame and tape the spike inside the collar strip, at the back.

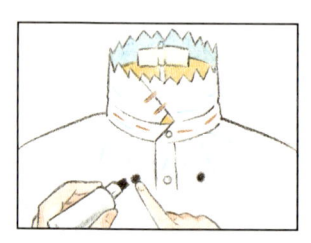

5. Fasten the top buttons and put the shirt and frame over your head. Mark where your eyes are with felt-tip. Take off and cut out eye holes.

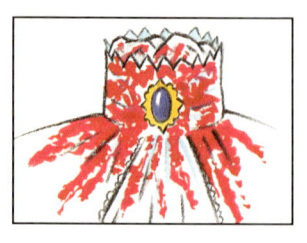

6. Crumple paper to fill the open neck. Gather the lace or doily and pin it on with a brooch. Dab the shirt with red paint mixed with glue.

76

Put rubber bands over sleeves near wrists to gather.

Paint ragged ends of sleeves with 'blood'.

To disguise the eye holes, glue white net over them on the inside and paint with 'blood'. You will still be able to see.

Tuck tracksuit bottoms inside boots.

See how to make head on next page.

Wrap long piece of material, or long scarf, around waist and tie at the side for a sash.

Tape a long edge of the black material or felt inside each boot top. Then fold down to the outside.

To put it on

Put on the white T-shirt and tracksuit bottoms. Tuck T-shirt in.

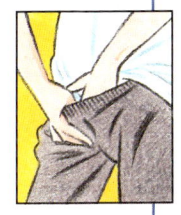

Attach sticky tabs to the inside of the shirt, around the eye holes.

Fasten the top two shirt buttons. Put the frame on your head.

Fasten the rest of the buttons from the outside (or get help).

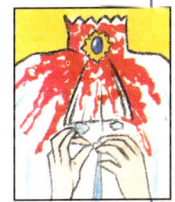

Press the sticky tabs gently to your face to hold in place.

Put your arms down the shirt sleeves. Cut seams more if you need to.

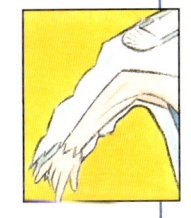

Tuck the big shirt neatly inside the tracksuit bottoms.

See next page for head.

77

Headless man's head

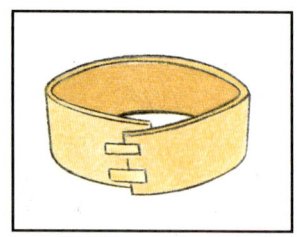

1. Bend the cardboard 8 x 40cm (3 x 16in) into a circle. Overlap the ends by 3cm (1in) and tape. This is the neck.

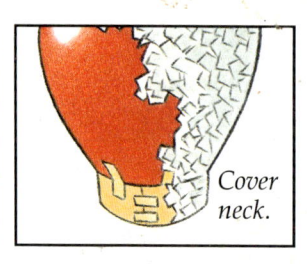

2. Blow the balloon up and knot it. Tape it, knot down, into the neck. Glue 3-4cm (1-1½in) squares of newspaper all over it. *Cover neck.*

3. Paint glue on top of the squares and add more until you have about four layers. When it is dry, cut the neck into points.

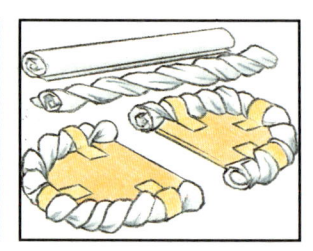

4. Cut two cardboard ears. Turn one over to make a left and a right ear. Twist pieces of paper to tape around ears. Tape the ears on.

Glue fringe of yarn for hair all around head.

Knot several long pieces of yarn together in the middle for moustache.

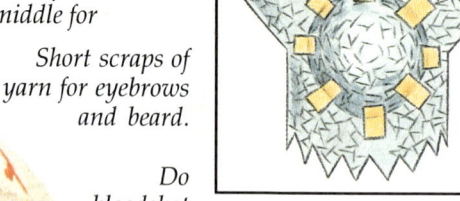

Short scraps of yarn for eyebrows and beard.

Do bloodshot eyes and pale, thin lips.

5. Crumple a little newspaper and wrap it in another piece to make a chin. Tape it to the bottom of the face, above the neck.

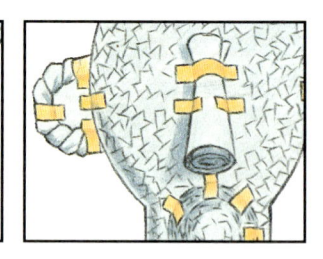

6. Roll up a strip of newspaper 10cm (4in) wide and tape it. Squash one end and tape it on for a nose. It may stick out.

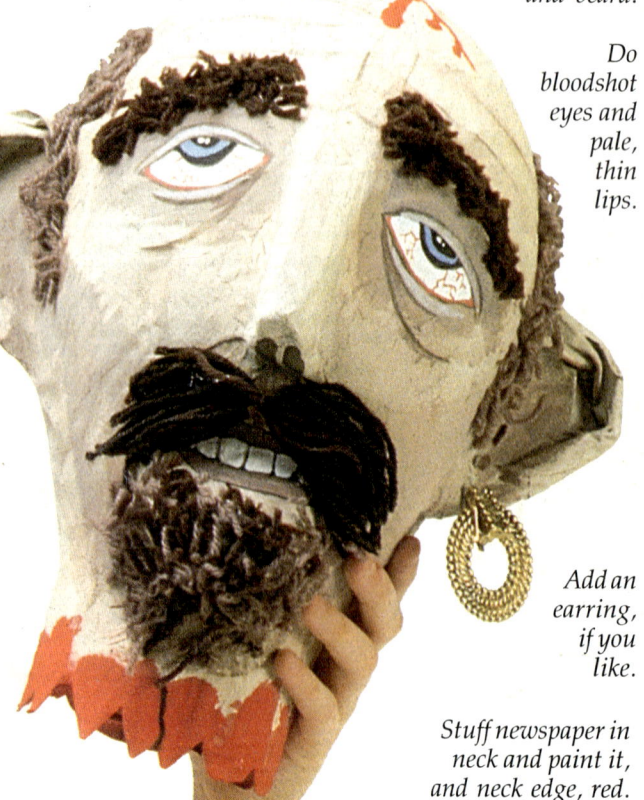

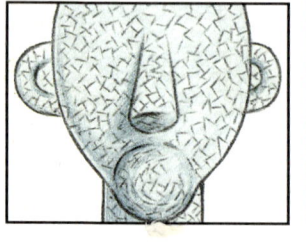

Add an earring, if you like.

Stuff newspaper in neck and paint it, and neck edge, red.

7. Glue more squares over the ears, nose and chin to hide the joins and attach firmly to the face. Use long strips over the nose.

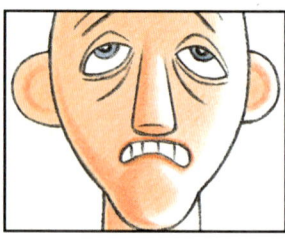

8. When dry, pop the balloon. Paint head in skin tone. Add eyes and a mouth. Glue on hair and beard as shown on the left.

Scarecrow

For this scarecrow, collect all the things listed on page 92, then put them together like this.

Carrot nose

Make a cone from stiff paper, 18 x 26cm (7 x 10in). Follow steps 1-3 on page 88. Wind it tightly for a slim cone. Make holes for elastic to fit around your head. Paint it like a carrot.

Wear gloves.

Tie a bright scarf around your neck.

Putting it on

Put on the T-shirt, trousers and jacket. Hold the trousers up with string.

Wrap a straw band (see above) inside each sleeve and trouser leg. Tie string around them.

Tape straw bands around the inside of the hat. Leave a space for your face.

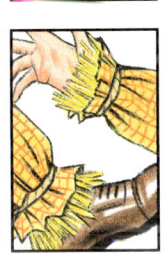

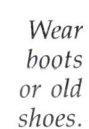

Wear boots or old shoes.

Put on carrot nose and hat last.

Straw bands

To make straw bands for the wrists, ankles and hat, sandwich pieces of straw between two lengths of tape.

Smudge your face with dirt. Or use face paints to paint it light brown with darker brown wrinkles.

Put a toy mouse or bird in top jacket pocket.

Knot string around trouser legs above knees.

Stuff a bright handkerchief in a side pocket.

Glue or sew bright patches onto trousers.

79

Superhero

This Superhero and the Superheroine on page 82 share many costume pieces. See how to make their belt, cuffs and breastplate here, and the cloak on page 83. Superhero also has a mask and Superheroine a headband. See page 93 for materials.

Basics: matching sweatshirt and tracksuit bottoms; trainers; thick socks.
To make: breastplate; belt; mask; cuffs; cloak.

Breastplate

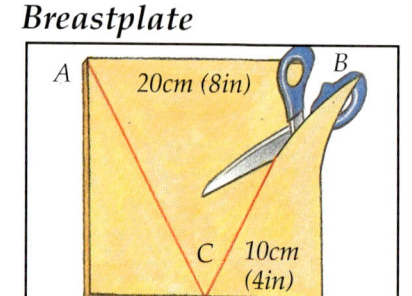

1. Cut a square of thin cardboard 20 x 20cm (8 x 8in). Mark half way along one side (C). Draw lines, then cut, from A and B to C.

2. Cut a piece of thick cardboard 9 x 8cm (3½ x 3in). Draw your initial really big on it and cut it out. Cut out the middle of the letter, too.

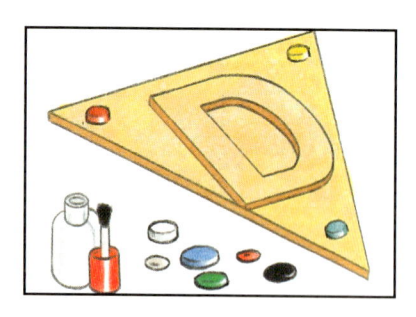

Letter cut out.

3. Glue the letter onto the breastplate, like this. Glue on small things, such as buttons and bottle tops, in a pattern and let it all dry.

4. Cut a piece of kitchen foil bigger than the breastplate. Cover the breastplate with glue and press the foil over it. Start in the middle.

Press into all the shapes.

Find out how to make the cloak on page 83.

5. Rub all the flat parts with a soft cloth to smooth and polish them. When it is dry, trim the foil to overlap by about 1cm (½in) all around.

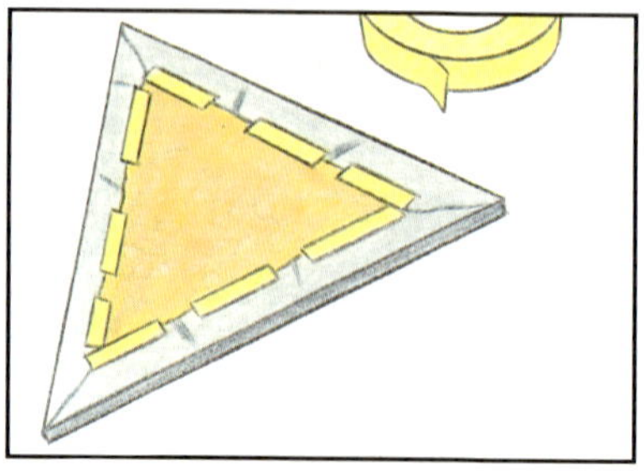

6. Turn the breastplate over. Fold the edges of the foil to the back and tape down. See how to give the foil an 'old' silver effect on page 83.

Wear thick socks that contrast with the basic outfit. Roll them down to your ankles.

All these accessories have been given the 'old' silver effect (see page 83).

See how to put on the whole outfit on page 83.

Superhero's mask

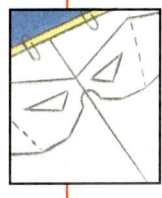

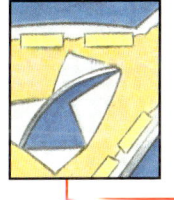

Trace the mask template on page 96 onto thin cardboard 30 x 9 cm (12 x 3½in). Cut it out, glue and cover with foil. Make snips in the eyes, fold flaps to the back and tape. Add elastic (page 94).

Making the belt

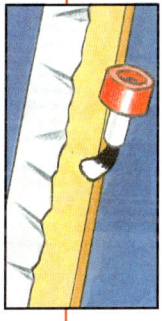

Cut a piece of thin cardboard 80 x 7cm (32 x 3in), and foil 1cm (½in) bigger. Glue the cardboard and stick on the foil. Fold the overlaps back and tape.

Cut a small, cardboard triangle, add a cardboard initial and cover with foil, as for the breastplate. Glue it to the middle of the belt.

Cuffs

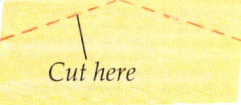

Cut here

Take thin cardboard 22 x 15cm (8½ x 6in). Cut one long side into a point. Glue, and cover with foil. Make two.

Superheroine

Basics: plain, bright swimsuit; clashing tights and long-sleeved T-shirt; contrasting knee socks; trainers or gym shoes.
To make: breastplate; belt; cuffs. (See how to make these three on pages 80-81.) Headband; cloak See page 93 for list.

Headband

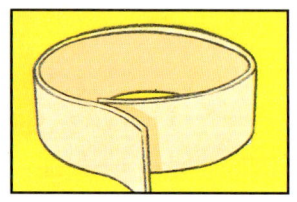

Take thin cardboard 9cm (3½in) wide and long enough to wrap around your head and overlap.

Mark the middle. Point

Cut along one long edge to make the band narrow at each end and come to a point in the middle.

Cut the same shape in foil, but 1cm (½in) bigger. Glue foil to the cardboard, fold back the overlap and tape.

Make breastplate, belt and cuffs as for Superhero (pages 80-81).

Wrap headband around head, overlap and tape.

Make a shorter cloak than Superhero's, if you like.

See page opposite for how to put accessories on.

You could decorate your face with face paint or self-adhesive stars.

Scrunch your socks down to your ankles.

Wear the swimsuit over tights and T-shirt.

82

Cloak

Use silky material, 100 x 90cm (39 x 36in). Lining material is good. It is shiny and comes in bright shades, often 90cm (36in) wide.

Twist rubber bands around two corners at each end of a short edge. Attach them about 12cm (4in) in. This gathers the cloth.

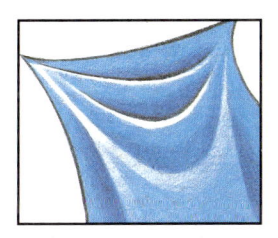

'Old' silver

Turn your accessories into 'old' silver by painting them with a mixture of black poster paint and glue that is not too thick.

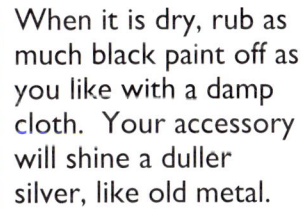

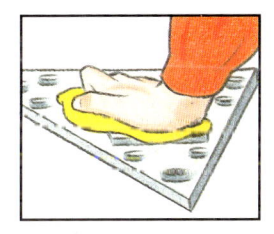

When it is dry, rub as much black paint off as you like with a damp cloth. Your accessory will shine a duller silver, like old metal.

Putting on the costumes

When you put on the Superhero or Superheroine costume, put on the basics first. Tuck in Superhero's sweatshirt, and make sure Superheroine's tights and T-shirt are stretched smoothly under the swimsuit. Stick in the shoulder pads. Then ask someone to help you put on the accessories you have made, as shown in the pictures below.

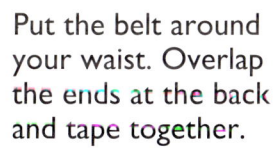

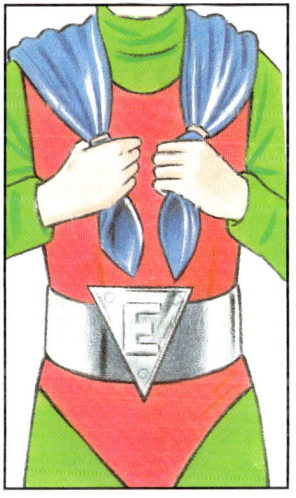

Points up outside of arms.

Tape under wrist.

Put the belt around your waist. Overlap the ends at the back and tape together.

Bring the ends of the cloak over your shoulders and safety pin to your chest.

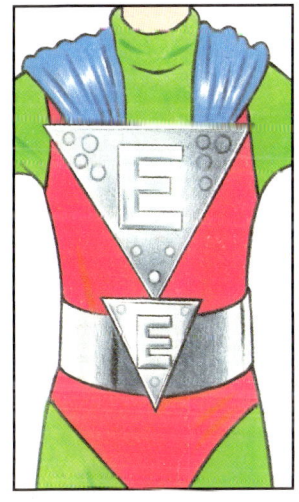

Place the breastplate over the ends of the cloak. Staple or sticky tab it into position.

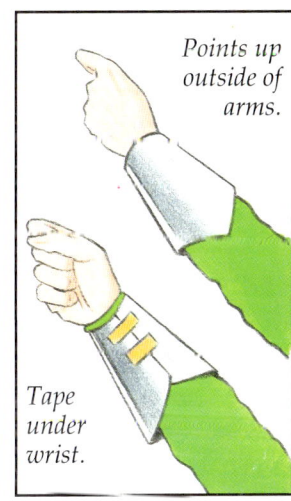

Bend the cuffs around your wrists, overlap and tape. Put on the mask or headband.

83

More heroes

These costumes use the same accessories as the Superhero and Superheroine. You can change the shape of the breastplate and add new things, such as a mask, tunic or hood, for more hero characters, like these.

Space Lord and Ghostly Warrior

Basics: black sweatshirt and tights or tracksuit bottoms; thick black socks; black shoes.

To make: belt; cuffs; breastplate; cloak. (See how to make these on pages 80-83.) Tunic; mask for Space Lord. Tunic; hood for Ghostly Warrior. See what you need on page 93.

Purple is good for the cloak.

Paint a ghostly face (page 15). Sling a toy sword in an extra belt.

Space Lord wears extra belt, black gloves and a ring of twisted foil.

Cut Ghostly Warrior's cloak and tunic into tatters.

Tunic

You need some silky material, twice as long as you are from shoulders to ankles and as wide as you across the shoulders.

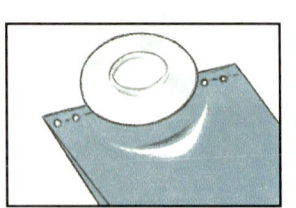

Fold the short sides together. Pin the fold. Place a small plate half on and half off the material, in the middle of the fold.

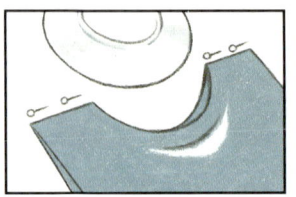

Draw around the half plate with a black felt-tip pen. Cut out the shape. Remove the pins. Try it over your head to see if it fits.

Space Lord's Mask

Trace and cut out the shapes on page 95 in thin cardboard. Stick the flashes onto the mask, then cover with glue and kitchen foil with 1cm (½in) overlap to fold back. Add cardboard strips to go around your head.

Hood

Fold the short ends of the thin, black material together.

Staple along one long side, turn inside out, then put on your head.

Tuck the ends into the neck of the sweatshirt and ease into shape.

Mad scientist

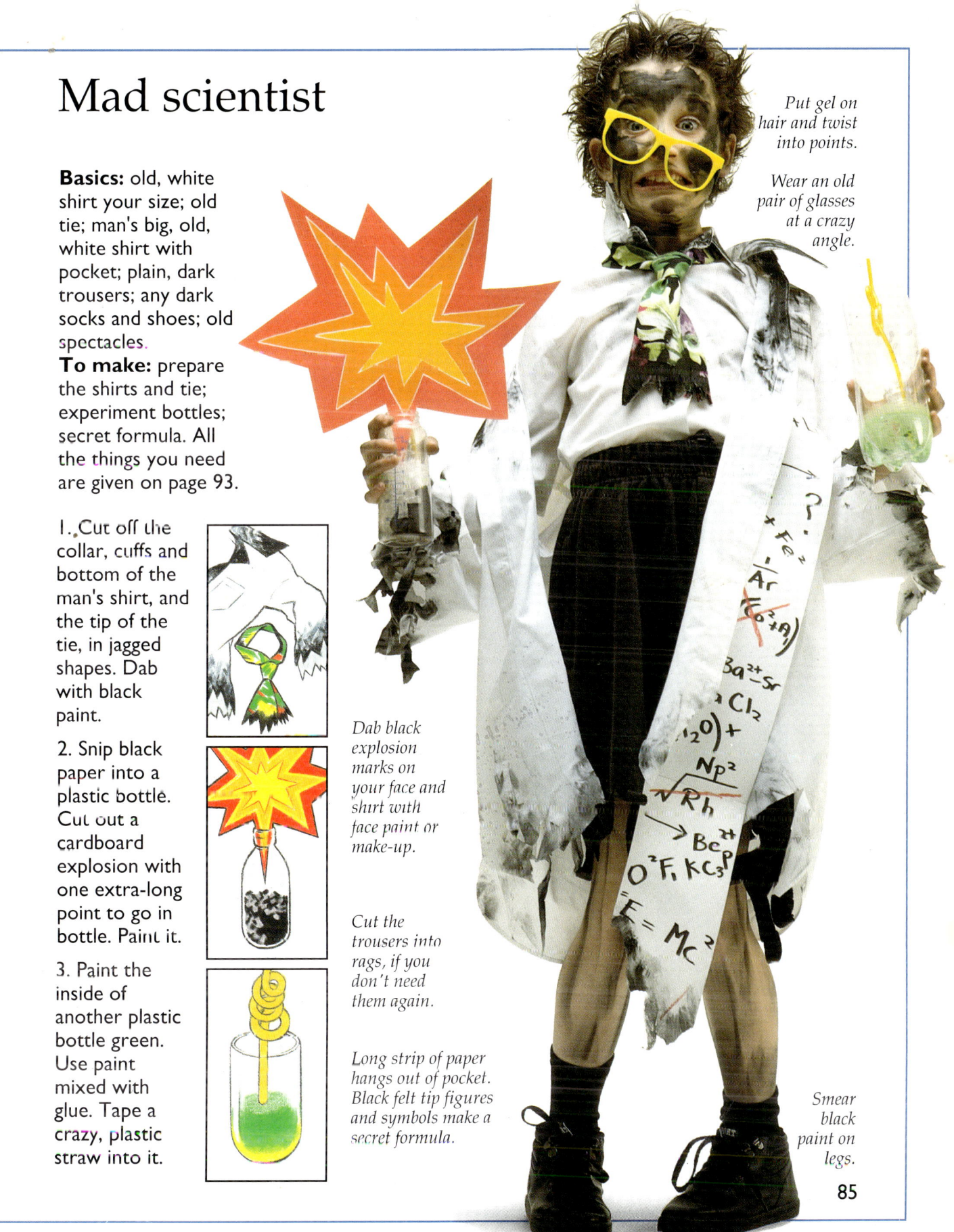

Basics: old, white shirt your size; old tie; man's big, old, white shirt with pocket; plain, dark trousers; any dark socks and shoes; old spectacles.

To make: prepare the shirts and tie; experiment bottles; secret formula. All the things you need are given on page 93.

1. Cut off the collar, cuffs and bottom of the man's shirt, and the tip of the tie, in jagged shapes. Dab with black paint.

2. Snip black paper into a plastic bottle. Cut out a cardboard explosion with one extra-long point to go in bottle. Paint it.

3. Paint the inside of another plastic bottle green. Use paint mixed with glue. Tape a crazy, plastic straw into it.

Put gel on hair and twist into points.

Wear an old pair of glasses at a crazy angle.

Dab black explosion marks on your face and shirt with face paint or make-up.

Cut the trousers into rags, if you don't need them again.

Long strip of paper hangs out of pocket. Black felt tip figures and symbols make a secret formula.

Smear black paint on legs.

85

Space monster

Basics: big, old, black sweatshirt and tracksuit bottoms; black socks, gym shoes and gloves; any T-shirt.
To make: mask; tail; paint body.

Mask

Fold

1. Trace and cut out the shapes on page 95 in stiff, black paper. Paint a design on half the mask in dark green paint.

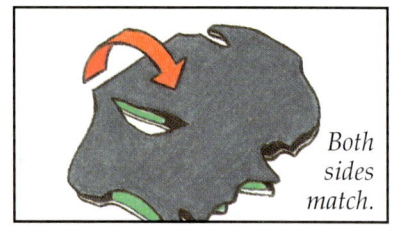

Both sides match.

To put mask on, hold it to your face and ask someone to bend strips around your head and tape at back. Put mask on last.

Find all the materials you need on page 93.

You could paint a monster face (pages 16-17); or use a mask from pages 52-53.

Wear black gloves.

For how to wash the paint off these clothes, see page 94.

For feelers, make holes through single sections of egg cartons. Poke pipecleaners through and bend to keep in place. Paint black. Twist other end around fingers.

2. Fold the mask along the fold line, press, then open out to blot pattern on both sides. Repeat with pale green paint. Do the same on the muzzle.

Changing shape
Put on a T-shirt. Hold sponges or egg cartons on your shoulders. Ask for help to tape them on as huge shoulder pads. Tape all the way around under your armpits.

Muzzle bends out from mask.

Tabs point in.

3. Outline one eye with red paint. Fold the mask to blot it on the other eye. Paint red teeth and nostrils on the muzzle. Let it dry.

4. Bend back the tabs on the muzzle and fold the ends under 2½cm (1in). Glue the ends flat onto the front of the mask, near the bottom.

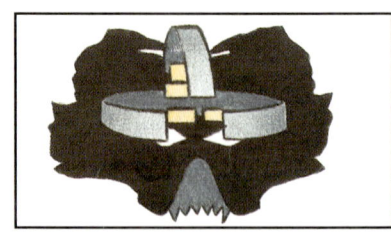

5. Tape the strips of cardboard 4 x 30cm (2 x 12in) onto the back of the mask, like this, and make them curve back.

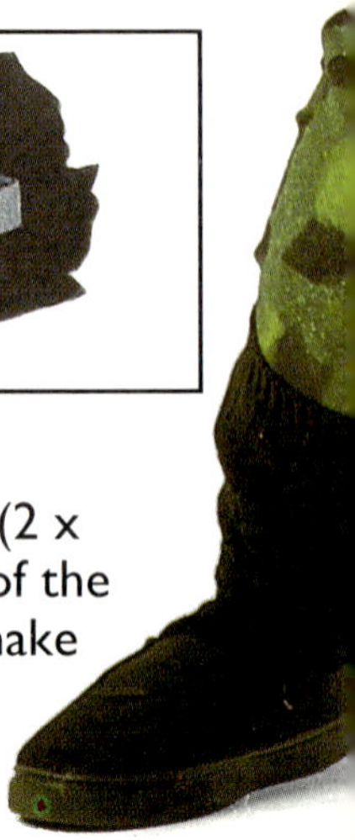

86

Body

1. Lay the sweatshirt on newspaper. Blot one half with dark green poster paint.

2. Quickly fold shirt in half from side to side. Press with a rolling pin. Repeat with pale green.

3. Do the same on the bottoms. Paint one leg, fold it on top of the other and press.

Tie tail to wrist with thread.

Tail

Cut off one leg of the tights and stuff with crumpled newspaper. Tie the open end with strong, black thread.

Mix green paint and glue on a plate. Press a crumpled rag into the paint and dab all over the tail.

Pin tail to back of trousers from the inside with a large safety pin.

Wear monster sweatshirt on top of T-shirt and shoulder pads.

Roll socks down.

Paint spikes black.

Cut a sponge into triangles for spikes. Glue and pin to end of tail.

87

Wizard

Basics: red tights, or tracksuit bottoms with red socks; red sweatshirt.
To make: tunic; hat; medallion; wand; hair; beard; moustache.

Tunic

Make a tunic in thin, red, material. Follow the steps on page 84 using measurements from page 93.

Hat

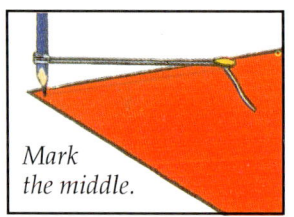

Mark the middle.

1. Tie string to a pencil and hold it at one corner of the red paper. Stretch and pin the string to the middle of a long edge.

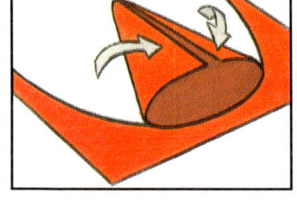

2. Draw a half-circle to the other corner (keep the string stretched). Cut it out. Bend the corners down toward the curved edge.

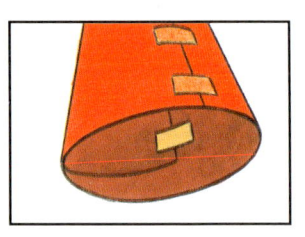

3. Overlap the corners until the paper forms a cone that fits your head. Paper clip together. Tape to hold.

4. On thin cardboard, trace and cut out the star on page 95. Fold the red, shiny paper into lots of layers.

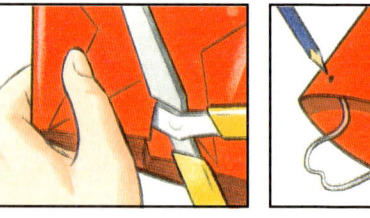

5. Draw around the star onto the paper. Cut out the shape to get lots of stars. Stick them onto the hat.

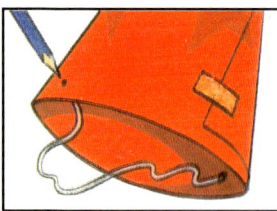

6. Poke holes at each side of the hat with a pencil. Thread with elastic to fit under your chin.

Wand

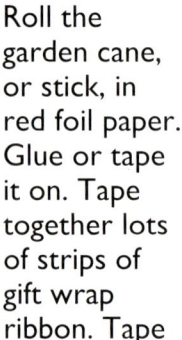

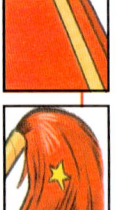

Roll the garden cane, or stick, in red foil paper. Glue or tape it on. Tape together lots of strips of gift wrap ribbon. Tape to one end.

Beard, moustache and hair

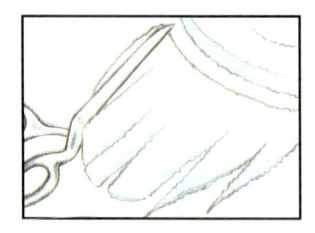

1. Cut wadding 19 x 23cm (7½ x 9in). Cut a teardrop shape out of it. Snip a curve in the top. Cut strips in it. Tease into points.

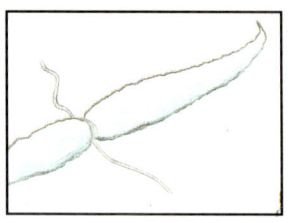

2. Cut more wadding 2 x 32cm (1 x 13in). Tie white thread around the middle. Tease the ends into points for moustache.

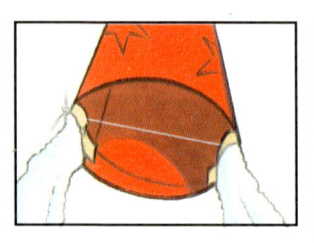

3. Cut two pieces of wadding 4 x 30cm (2 x 12in). Cut two thirds of the way up each. Tape in the hat 12cm (5in) apart.

To put on

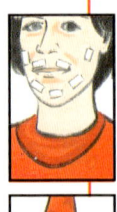

Put on basic costume and tunic. Put sticky tabs on dry skin, as shown. Press on beard and moustache. Add the medallion and hat.

88

Medallion

Glue top of margarine tub lid and cover with foil. Trim to 2cm (1in), fold edges to back and tape.

Roll strips of foil and bend around the gumdrops. Twist ends together and snip off extra.

Glue the lid and press gumdrops on it in a pattern. Snip pieces of gumdrop to fill the gaps.

Paint thickly all over the lid with glue. It looks cloudy at first, but dries clear.

Twist lots of foil strips. Tape to the back, all around the lid. Bend into curly shapes.

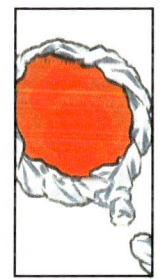

You could make wadding eyebrows, too.

You could put wrinkles around eyes with make-up or face paint.

Stick extra stars to the strips on the wand, if you like.

Put wadding all around hat, if you want to.

Stick silver ribbon to back of medallion to hang around your neck.

You can stick medallion to tunic with sticky tabs to stop it from swinging.

Glue shiny stars or pin brooches to front of tunic, if you like.

Comic waiter

This waiter has a magic tray that never spills, but people don't know that if you pretend to tip it at them.

Basics: black jacket and trousers; white shirt; bow tie; black shoes and socks; white gloves; large, white, cloth napkin.
To make: jacket tails; tray. See page 93.

Tails

Cut a long triangle of black material in half, like this.

Sew or staple the pieces to the back edge of the jacket.

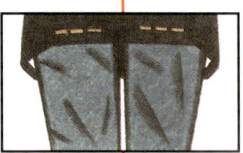

Put all the basics on first. Put the bow tie and gloves on last.

You could paint on a curly moustache with face paint.

If you put a napkin on the tray, use an old one, as you have to glue it on.

You could use the same joke tray with a waitress's costume.

Ask someone to put sticky tabs on the gloved hand you want to hold the tray with. Get them to press the tray on firmly.

Make a flower (see right) to put in your buttonhole, or pin to your lapel.

To make the tray

Wash and dry half an empty egg shell. Paint it carefully inside and out with glue.

Stick the egg shell onto a plastic egg cup. Glue the egg cup to a paper plate.

You can dip a white flower in red paint to dye the tips of the petals.

Gel hair and part in the middle.

Add light things to the tray, such as plastic cutlery and a paper napkin, if you like. A flower is a *nice touch*.

Pretend to trip and spill the tray. It will stay firmly stuck to your hand.

Carry the cloth napkin over one arm. Hold it there with sticky tabs.

The more horrified you look at 'spilling' the tray, the better the joke is.

Making flowers

Cut a long strip of tissue paper about 8cm (3in) wide. Snip all along one edge.

Roll up the strip and tape the end. Gently pull out and spread the snips for petals.

Make a slice of toast. When cold, cut into four, paint with glue and stick to the plate.

Put cornflakes into a paper bowl. Mix them with glue to stick them together.

Paint inside a clear, plastic glass with white paint and glue. Tape in a straw.

Glue the white cloth to the tray. Arrange and glue on all the things you have made.

91

Shopping lists

Check you have all you need from these lists before you start.

Clown p.66-67

Tape or stapler
Several bright felt squares
2 paper cups
Darning needle and bright yarn
4 safety pins
Sharp pencil
Two sided sticky tabs
2 pieces of wide, bright ribbon 1m (1yd) in length
White cardboard 45 x 7cm (18 x 3in)
Red crepe paper
Orange and another bright tissue paper
Self-adhesive stars and spots
Face paints or make-up
Basics: Bright T-shirt, man's big, old trousers, white gloves, bright tights, clashing socks, trainers or gym shoes, hat.

Black-and-white cat p.68-69

Greaseproof or tracing paper
Thin black fur fabric 70 x 30cm (28 x 12in)
Medium wadding 35 x 25cm (14 x 10in)
Thin black cardboard 23 x 15cm (9½ x 6½in)
Thin white cardboard 12 x 6cm (5 x 2½in)
PVA glue
Stapler
Scissors
Black face paint (optional)
Ballpoint pen, pencil, felt-tip pen
Dressmaking pins
8 safety pins
Strong black thread

Black shirring elastic 55cm (22in) and 25cm (10in)
Kitchen foil
Basics: black sweatshirt and thick tights or tracksuit bottoms, thick, white socks, white gloves.

Giant vampire bat p.70

Large, black plastic bag
Rubber band
Tracing paper and pencil
Tape measure
Dressmaking pins
Needle and black thread
Scissors, clear tape
Ballpoint pen
Black felt 24 x 28cm (10 x 12in)
Old pair of thick, black tights
Face paint or joke vampire teeth
Basics: black sweatshirt, tracksuit bottoms, socks, gloves and gym shoes.

Butterfly p.71

Dressmaking pins
Pastel net, the length you are from wrist to wrist with your arms stretched out to your sides, and 80cm (32in) long.
Scraps of silky material
Things to draw around, such as a plate or glass
Felt-tip pen, scissors
Fine white shirring elastic
Headband
2 fluffy pipe cleaners
Needle and thread
Face paints or make-up
Basics: pastel leotard or swimsuit, pretty, contrasting tights, ballet shoes or slippers.

Skeleton p.72-73

Black and white poster paint and thick brush
Small decorator's paintbrush
Old newspapers
Clear tape
Needle and black thread
2 large safety pins
2 small plastic bags
Thin white cardboard 3 x 21cm (1 x 8in)
Kitchen foil, PVA glue
Black and white face paints or skull mask.
Basics: old, black, hooded sweatshirt and tracksuit bottoms ironed flat (both to fit as tightly as possible), with socks; or thick, black tights; black, washable gloves.

Boxer p.74

2 squares white felt 10 x 10cm (4 x 4in)
2 small safety pins
Ruler, scissors, clear tape
Stapler, double-sided tape
Small margarine tub lid (any shape), kitchen foil
Thin black cardboard 80 x 6cm (32 x 2½in)
80cm (32in) blue ribbon and white ribbon, both 1cm (½in) wide
80cm (32in) gold or yellow fringing or braid
PVA glue and brush
Picture of a boxer
Black felt-tip pen, pencil
Clean, dry cloth, hair gel
Face paint or eyeshadow
Basics: plain, bright dressing gown, shorts to match, black or white gym shoes or trainers, white laces, sports socks, two bandages (any kind), shoulder pads.

Back-to-front person p.75

Face mask, optional wig
White paper, poster paints
Fine sandpaper
PVA glue, clear tape
Basics: Shirt, tie, jacket, skirt, socks or tights, shoes.

Headless man p.76-78

1 wire coathanger
1 pair shoulder pads
Foam bath sponge 14 x 11cm (5½ x 4in)
Stapler, PVA glue, clear tape, two sided sticky tabs
Red paint and paintbrush
Felt-tip pen, scissors
Thin cardboard 60 x 5cm (24 x 2in), 2 rubber bands
Piece white lace or doily
Long piece of narrow, material or scarf for sash
Man's big, old, white shirt
2 pieces black material or felt 52 x 17cm (22 x 7in)
Old newspaper
For the head:
1 round balloon
Thin cardboard 8 x 40cm (3 x 16in), and 2 pieces 9 x 5cm (3½ x 2in)
Old newspaper, clear tape
Poster paints and brush
Brown or black yarn
Basics: black tracksuit bottoms, white T-shirt, black boots, big brooch.

Scarecrow p.79

Thick string
Bright scraps of material
Straw (from pet shops)
Clear tape
Sheet of stiff paper and orange poster paint
Shirring elastic
Face paints or make-up

Basics: T-shirt (any kind), large, old jacket and trousers, boots or old shoes, gloves, bright scarf and handkerchief, old hat, toy mouse or bird.

Superhero p.80-81

Coat lining material to contrast with basics, 100 x 90cm (39 x 36in)
25cm (10in) shirring elastic
Stapler, paperclips, PVA glue, clear tape
3 safety pins
2 small rubber bands
1 pair shoulder pads
Damp cloth, old saucer
Black poster paint and paintbrush
Greaseproof or tracing paper, pencils
Thin cardboard in these sizes: 20 x 20cm (8 x 8in), 80 x 7cm (32 x 3in), 15 x 15cm (6 x 6in), 30 x 9cm (12 x 3½in), two pieces 15 x 17cm (6 x 7in)
Thick cardboard 9 x 8cm (3½ x 3in)
Kitchen foil, scissors, ruler
Bottle tops, buttons etc.
Soft, dry cloth
Basics: matching sweatshirt and tracksuit bottoms, gym shoes or trainers, socks.

Superheroine p.82-83

As for Superhero, plus:
Thin cardboard 9 x 30cm (3½ x 12in)
Basics: plain, bright swimsuit, clashing tights and long-sleeved T-shirt, contrasting knee socks, trainers or gym shoes.

Space lord p.84

As for Superhero, plus: black coat lining material for the tunic: as wide as your shoulders and twice as long as from your neck to feet.
Small plate
Black felt-tip pen
Dressmaking pins
Thin cardboard 31 x 28cm (13 x 12in) and 2 strips 4 x 30cm (2 x 12in)
Kitchen foil
Basics: black sweatshirt and thick tights or tracksuit bottoms, black socks, gloves, gym shoes or trainers, leather belts.

Ghostly warrior p.84

As for Superhero, plus: grey coat lining for tunic (same as Space lord's)
Thin, black material 53 x 90cm (22 x 36in)
Face paints or skull mask.
Basics: as for Space lord, plus toy sword.

Mad scientist p.85

2 plastic bottles
Black felt-tip pen
Crazy straw
Piece thin, white cardboard, poster paints, PVA glue
Scraps of black paper
Long strip of paper
Face paints or make-up
Hair gel
Basics: old, white shirt to fit you, old tie, old trousers (not jeans), big, old, man's white shirt, old spectacles, dark socks and shoes.

Space monster p.86-87

Tracing paper and pencil
2 large sponges or cardboard egg cartons
Stiff black paper 38 x 50cm (16 x 21in)
3 pieces stiff, black paper 4 x 30cm (2 x 12in)
clear tape, PVA glue
2 paper clips
Green and red poster paint and big paintbrush
Old plate (to mix paint)
Rolling pin
For the tail:
Sponge
Old, thick, black tights
Old newspapers, rag
Strong, black thread
Large safety pin, sponge
For feelers:
Ten pipe cleaners
Ten cardboard egg carton segments
Black paint
Basics: T-shirt (any kind), big, old, black sweatshirt and tracksuit bottoms (ironed flat), black gloves and long socks, black gym shoes.

Wizard p.88-89

Thin red material twice as long as you are from neck to feet and as wide as from elbow to elbow (hold your arms out to the sides to measure).
Medium wadding 29 x 32cm (11½ x 13in).
Stiff red paper 70 x 77cm (29 x 32in)
Pencil
Thin string 45cm (19in) long
70cm (29in) silver ribbon
Sheet red, shiny paper
Greaseproof or tracing paper
Scissors,
Thin cardboard
White thread
Garden cane or stick
Two sided sticky tabs, clear tape, PVA glue
Round plastic food tub lid
Kitchen foil
White shirring elastic
Large, red gumdrops
Roll of narrow, shiny, red gift wrap ribbon.
Basics: red sweatshirt, red tights, or tracksuit bottoms with red socks, glittery brooches.

Comic waiter p.90-91

Black material 42 x 44cm (17½ x 18½in) cut into a long triangle
Hair gel
Face paint or make-up
Sheet bright tissue paper
Sticky tabs
Black thread and a needle, or a stapler
For the tray:
Square of white cloth, or old, cloth napkin, to cover the tray, and hang over
Paper plate and bowl
Plastic egg-cup
Transparent plastic glass
Straw
Egg shell, slice of bread, cornflakes
White paint, PVA glue, clear tape
Basics: black jacket and trousers, socks and shoes, white shirt and gloves, bow tie on elastic, white cloth napkin (for over arm).

Templates

Templates are shapes you draw around. You need to trace them from the book to use them. Some are whole templates and some are half templates. You trace these in different ways, which are explained here.

Usually, you transfer the shapes onto paper or cardboard, as described in the steps here; but sometimes you use the shape as a pattern. This means you cut it out and put it on top of material or paper, pin it on or draw around it, then cut the shape out. It tells you on the template if you need to do this.

To trace half templates

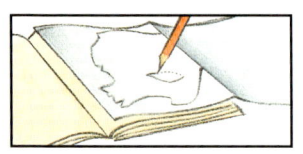

1. Fold tracing paper in half, then open it. Put it over the template, with the crease matching the edge of the page. Trace the shape.

2. Take the tracing off and re-fold it. Turn it over. Draw over the outline you can see to complete the shape. Open out, then follow steps 2 and 3 below.

To trace templates

1. Put tracing paper over the template. Hold in place with paper clips. Draw over the outline with a soft, dark pencil.

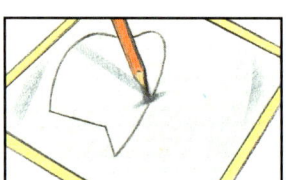

2. Turn the tracing paper over. Put it on the cardboard you are using and go over the shape again with a hard, sharp pencil.

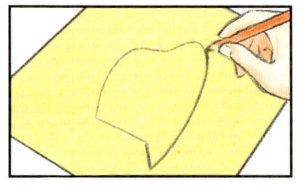

3. Go over the faint lines this leaves with pencil (use a white crayon on black paper or cardboard). Cut out the shape.

Washing clothes

If you paint clothes that you want to wear again, let them soak in cold water. This helps lift paint out of them. Rinse and squeeze out. Then wash in a machine as usual. Do not mix paint with glue if you want to wash it out.

Eye holes

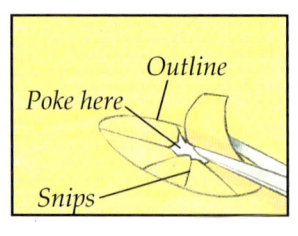

Poke a pencil or pen into the eye hole. Put a scissor blade into the hole and make snips to the eye outline. Cut around the outline last.

Elastic holes

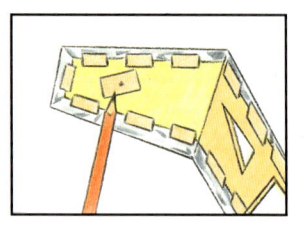

Make small holes with a sharp pencil. They will be stronger if you put a small square of tape over them, then pierce again. Thread elastic.

Press the pages as flat as you can to trace over the fold in the middle.

94

This dotted line is where teeth end.

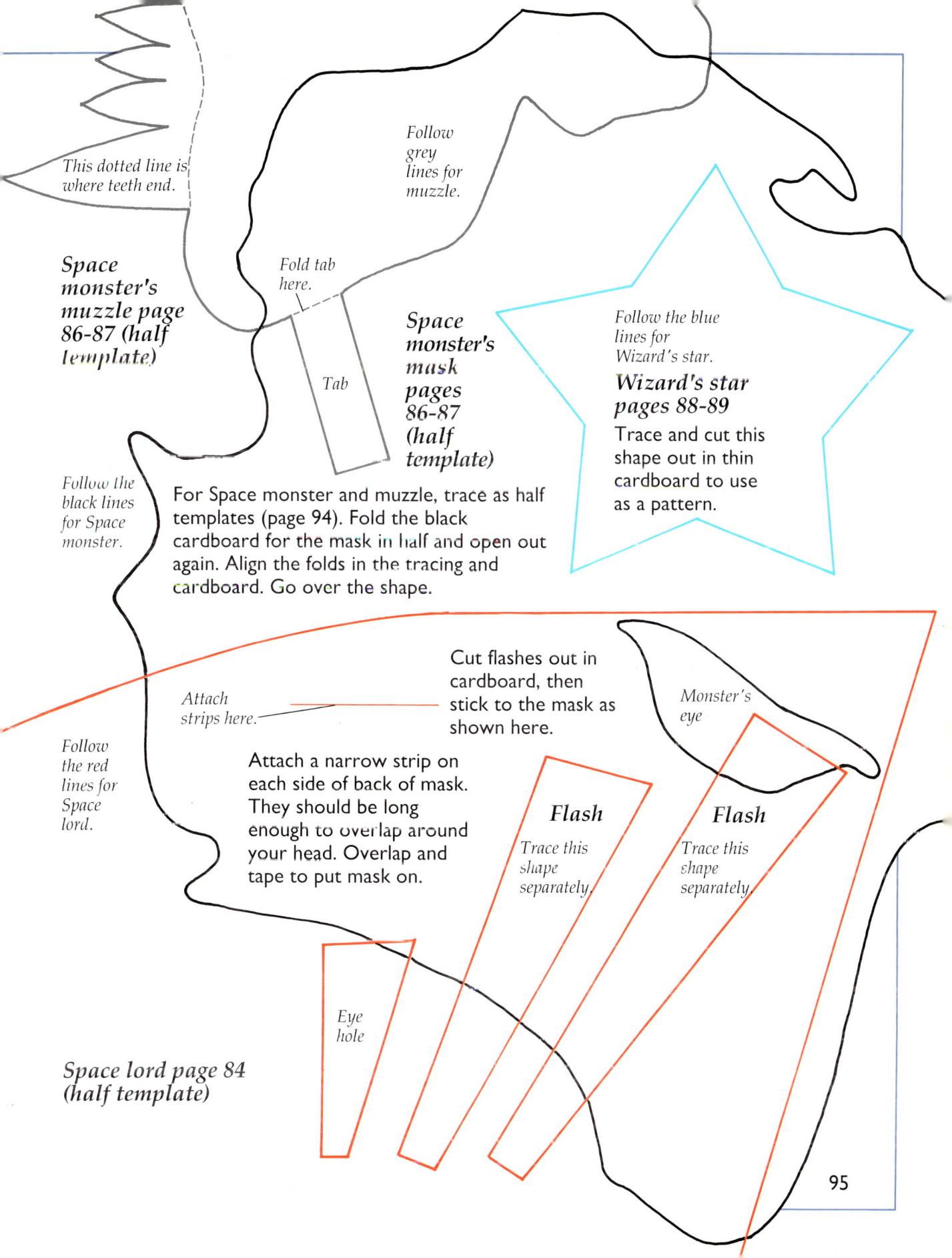

Space monster's muzzle page 86-87 (half template)

Follow grey lines for muzzle.

Fold tab here.

Tab

Space monster's mask pages 86-87 (half template)

Follow the blue lines for Wizard's star.

Wizard's star pages 88-89

Trace and cut this shape out in thin cardboard to use as a pattern.

Follow the black lines for Space monster.

For Space monster and muzzle, trace as half templates (page 94). Fold the black cardboard for the mask in half and open out again. Align the folds in the tracing and cardboard. Go over the shape.

Attach strips here.

Cut flashes out in cardboard, then stick to the mask as shown here.

Monster's eye

Follow the red lines for Space lord.

Attach a narrow strip on each side of back of mask. They should be long enough to overlap around your head. Overlap and tape to put mask on.

Flash
Trace this shape separately.

Flash
Trace this shape separately.

Eye hole

Space lord page 84 (half template)

Elastic hole ○

Superhero's mask pages 80-81 (half template)

Eye hole

Bend mask sides back at dotted line.

Follow the black lines for Superhero's mask.

Cat's ear pages 68-69

Trace this shape twice, then cut out of the tracing paper. Turn one over for a right and a left ear.

Fold smaller part of ear toward larger part at dotted line. Fold opposite ways for right and left ear.

Follow the red lines for cat's mask and ear.

Cat mask pages 68-69 (half template)

Mark for ear

Cat's brow
Trace separately.
You cut this shape from wadding. Trace it, then cut out to use as a pattern.

Mark for ear

Elastic hole ○

Eye hole

Bat's ear page 70

Trace this shape, then cut it out of the tracing paper, pin to black felt and cut around it. Turn one felt ear over to make a left and a right ear.

Cat's cheek
Trace separately.
You cut this shape from wadding. Trace it (page 94) then cut it out to use as a pattern.

Fold side of ear in from here.

Follow the blue lines for bat's ear.

96